# THE ROBIN HOOD RULES FOR SMART GIVING

# THE
# ROBIN HOOD
# RULES FOR SMART GIVING

## Michael M. Weinstein
## and Ralph M. Bradburd

Columbia Business School
Publishing

Columbia University Press
*Publishers Since 1893*
New York    Chichester, West Sussex
cup.columbia.edu

Library of Congress Cataloging-in-Publication Data
Weinstein, Michael M.
The Robin Hood rules for smart giving / Michael M. Weinstein
and Ralph M. Bradburd.
pages cm
ISBN 978-0-231-15836-7 (cloth : alk. paper) — ISBN 978-0-231-53524-3 (ebook)
1. Endowments. 2. Charities. 3. Robin Hood Foundation.
I. Bradburd, Ralph M. II. Title.

HV25.W353 2013
361.7068'4--dc23

2012050814

Cover design: Julia Kushnirsky
Cover image: The Robin Hood Foundation

# CONTENTS

# PREFACE

This book offers a framework, Relentless Monetization (RM), by which to measure the impact of philanthropic interventions. It provides a strategy for comparing the value of one philanthropic option against another—a strategy by which to make smart philanthropic decisions. The power of RM lies in its consistent and persistent application of benefit/cost analysis. Implemented carefully, the strategy takes full account of the funder's philanthropic mission, the preferences and values of nonprofit actors (funders, donors, policy makers, academics, service deliverers) and resources. RM also takes full account of the best available evidence about the impact of philanthropic interventions on the outcomes that are relevant to the missions of funders and donors. And the strategy does all this in a manner that leaves a tangible trail of accountability, thereby exposing philanthropic decisions to challenge and revision.

The book grounds the discussion of RM in the practice of the Robin Hood Foundation, the largest private charity dedicated to fighting poverty in New York City. One of the authors, Michael Weinstein, has been in charge of Robin Hood's grant making for the past ten years and in that role developed RM. The other author, Ralph Bradburd, has served as a consultant to Robin Hood. Given its central role in this book, a word about Robin Hood is in order. It aims to "find, fund and cultivate the most effective poverty-fighting methods and programs." Beyond cash grants, Robin Hood provides its grantees with management assistance—help solving real estate problems, adopting fiscal systems, developing marketing strategies, improving fund raising capacity, and building boards of directors. In 2012, Robin Hood made about $113 million in grants and other commitments to more than 200 poverty-fighting programs, directly serving hundreds of thousands of New York residents. Robin Hood's board pays all of the organization's administrative, fund raising, and evaluation costs, guaranteeing that 100 percent of every donation by non-board members goes directly to organizations serving low income New Yorkers.

The reader may wonder why RM has blossomed at Robin Hood. No mystery. Its founders and major donors come disproportionately from the hedge fund industry and other financial sectors. Many were "quants" trained to wallow in numbers. From the get-go in 1988, Robin Hood vowed to apply "investment principles" to the practice of philanthropy. Board members insisted that the Robin Hood staff invest their philanthropic dollars every bit as effectively as they invest their hedge fund dollars. The rhetorical commitment of Robin Hood's board led staff early on to collect extensive data. The board then brought in Michael Weinstein, an economist, to develop a rigorous system for making cost-effective philanthropic decisions.

The easy prediction would have been that trying to meld formal, quantitative, results-oriented investment strategies with philanthropic goals would be disruptive—and so it was, measured in terms of the processes for analyzing grant proposals and the content of grants. But the disruption did not trigger much resistance among staffers for the simple reason that the board had made Robin Hood's direction abundantly clear. The question became how, not whether, to formalize and quantify. Readers will judge for themselves to what extent the system that Robin Hood has adopted holds up to scrutiny.

Although the examples we use throughout the book are based on one author's experience at Robin Hood, we do not use actual names of grantees or their data.

For whom is this book written? RM is a framework for making choices among philanthropic options when resources are limited. Funders like Robin Hood make such choices. So do donors, nonprofits (community-based organizations), policy advocates, and policy makers. The RM framework is designed to guide all of these philanthropic actors. Given the role that Robin Hood's practice plays in this book, explicit reference is often made to decisions made by funders. But the discussion would follow precisely the same lines were it written from the point of view of nonprofits or other philanthropists.

Special acknowledgment goes to Cynthia E. Lamy, whose responsibilities at Robin Hood include finding and creatively interpreting research as the first step in applying the principles of RM to the practical task of assigning numerical value to hundreds of potential and actual antipoverty interventions. Her painstaking efforts populate the examples in chapters 6 and 7, which provide examples that bring theory into concrete form. We'd like to offer a personal shout out to David Saltzman, Robin Hood's visionary executive director, who gave the new economist in town a wide berth in which to build on his magnificent grant-making handiwork. That took guts. That took patience. That took character.

Finally we celebrate the oh-so-smart advice that Myles Thompson and Bridget Flannery-McCoy showered on us, patiently guiding our thoughts as we restructured, reorganized, and rewrote.

# THE ROBIN HOOD RULES FOR SMART GIVING

# 1

# Overview of Relentless Monetization

You're a philanthropist whose mission is to fight poverty. You're choosing between two different ways to allocate your charity. One option would have you donate $10 million to teach carpentry to female high school dropouts. A second option would have you donate $10 million to middle schools that serve disadvantaged children to expand their onsite psychological services. Which option do you choose?

This thought experiment triggers two questions. How can you, as a philanthropist, make the right choice? And what exactly does "right" mean in this context?

This book lays out a concise framework for answering these questions, a framework by which to make smart philanthropic decisions. By philanthropic decisions, we mean decisions driven by a mission other than the maximization of personal profit. By smart, we mean achieving philanthropic goals to the maximum extent possible with whatever money is available. We call our framework *Relentless Monetization (RM)*. It methodically applies the workhorse of modern economics, benefit/cost analysis, to the task of making effective philanthropic choices.

For many readers, "relentless" and "monetization" carry negative connotations. So why do we focus on them? Why do we argue that putting the two terms together makes for smart philanthropy? By monetization, we refer to assigning dollar values to philanthropic outcomes. And relentless means making these assignments even when the benefits associated with those outcomes are hard to measure and the evidentiary basis for assigning dollar values to specific outcomes is slim. RM uses these monetized values, however uncertain, to guide philanthropists toward their best, smartest options. RM, we argue, provides a reliable, transparent answer to the kind of question we posed in our opening thought experiment: Given my mission of fighting poverty, should I fund carpentry training for unemployed women or psychological counseling for middle school students?

To whom is this book directed? RM is all about analyzing philanthropic choices. As such, it informs the decisions of any actors who make such choices: donors, nonprofit organizations, government officials, legislators, policy experts, or anyone else facing philanthropic tradeoffs. In a world of finite resources, philanthropists cannot fund every activity that does good, not even every activity that does a lot of good. They must make choices. The idea behind this book is that philanthropists cannot settle for choosing programs merely because they generate important benefits. They must hold out for funding only those programs that do the *most* good per dollar of costs. Otherwise money is wasted, which is an unforgivable mistake given yawning social needs. The analysis would be largely the same no matter which actors would be in mind. Much of our discussion in this book is directed at "funders," but that's simply a mannerism. The discussion could just as easily be directed at the leaders of nonprofit organizations or any other philanthropic actors.

This book makes the case that, *as a matter of theory*, RM applies to philanthropic endeavors of all stripes. We could have posed the initial thought experiment from the point of view of environmentalists: Should they spend money to save oysters in the Chesapeake Bay or polar bears in the Arctic? Or we could have posed the thought experiment from the point of view of human rights activists: Should they focus their time and money on countering the trend in Latin America of electing authoritarians to political office, or on steering courts in the United States away from sentencing juvenile offenders to prison?

However widely the RM framework applies to philanthropic decision making in theory, the question arises of how widely applicable will the RM framework be *in practice*. Can it guide real-time philanthropic decisions in smart directions? To address this question, this book tracks the actual practices of the Robin Hood Foundation, a nonprofit that makes grants of about $120 million a year to community-based organizations in New York

City to alleviate poverty. One of the authors developed RM there as Robin Hood's chief program officer over the past decade.

It is on the basis of the examples set forth in this book that we claim that RM not only works in theory, but also in practice (at least for the purpose of guiding efforts to fight urban poverty). That said, the book by necessity leaves open the question of how well the framework will transfer to other philanthropic realms. For example, will environmentalists and human rights activists find the framework equally powerful? That question can be answered only as philanthropies of different stripes experiment with RM. We hope this book will stimulate philanthropic actors to adopt RM's principles in pursuit of their own missions. From such implementation, we'll learn exactly how generally applicable RM will prove to be.

Here's a quick note on terminology. We use the term "nonprofits" to refer to either (1): community-based organizations (soup kitchens) that provide direct services (emergency food) to targeted individuals to achieve a philanthropic goal (alleviate hunger); or to (2) the funders of such community-based organizations. Context dictates which meaning we have in mind.

## Seven Steps That Define Relentless Monetization

Recall the central questions posed by the previous thought experiment: Should a poverty fighting funder spend money on job training or middle school instruction? There is no obvious answer to questions like this, although RM provides a road map for proper scrutiny.

A basic problem that plagues philanthropic decisions is that there is no natural yardstick by which to measure, and therefore compare, different philanthropic outcomes. Said another way, there is no one natural way by which to compare, for the purpose of fighting poverty, the value of providing job training to a would-be carpenter to the value of providing better middle school instruction. Nor, similarly, is there one natural way to compare the value of saving oysters in the Chesapeake Bay to the value of saving polar bears in the Arctic. RM makes such comparisons possible and explicit.

Contrast philanthropy actors to garden variety for-profit actors. For-profit actors do share one natural yardstick: profit. To paraphrase Michael Boskin, chairman of President George H. W. Bush's Council of Economic Advisors, capitalists don't care whether they earn a dollar's worth of profit by selling potato chips or computer chips. Profit is profit. Success is measured the same way regardless of which product is sold. No novel yardstick is needed to compare the success of a potato chip factory with that of a computer chip factory. The central premise of this book is that RM offers philanthropic actors a common measuring rod by which to measure success of philanthropic outcomes, the analog to the role that profit plays in measuring success of for-profit activities.

We'll now briefly set out the seven steps that define RM. To make the exposition easy to swallow, we follow a concrete example through the seven-step process: Our example is that of a nonprofit whose mission is to fight poverty, making grants to educational programs that serve disadvantaged children. Each step is explained in depth in subsequent chapters.

*Step 1: Adopt a mission statement.*

Here, the mission is fighting poverty.

*Step 2: Translate the mission statement into well-defined goals.*

Here, translate the mission to "fight poverty" into the goal of improving the living standards of poor individuals by raising income and improving health.

Steps 1 and 2 define what the nonprofit deems important. The next steps determine how well individual activities (or "interventions") accomplish what the nonprofit deems important. Steps 3 through 6 sketch the process by which the nonprofit places a dollar value on single interventions.

*Step 3: Identify a specific intervention to analyze.*

The philanthropic intervention we envision throughout this book is a grant made by a funder to a nonprofit. Let's focus here on a grant to a middle school to expand onsite psychological services for currently enrolled students and create a college counseling service for recent graduates of the middle school who have since enrolled in high school or college.

*Step 4: Identify each and every mission-relevant outcome (MRO) that follows from the intervention. (Grants can generate one or more MROs.)*

Each MRO must satisfy two conditions. Condition 1: The outcome must be caused by the intervention identified in Step 2 (in the sense that if the intervention were removed, the outcome would disappear). Condition 2: The outcome must be tied to the mission according to Steps 1 and 2.

The hypothetical grant anticipates two mission-related outcomes. Does each of them satisfy the two conditions? In this case, the answer is yes.

Outcome 1: Boost high school graduation rates.

Condition 1: Onsite psychological services increase the probability that students graduate from high school. Condition 2: Over their careers graduates earn more than do demographically similar students who drop out of high school.

Outcome 2: College persistence.

Condition 1: Counseling helps college students handle problems that otherwise cause them to drop out. Condition 2: Every extra year of college enrollment increases future earnings on average.

*Step 5: Monetize—that is to say, assign a dollar value—to each outcome identified in Step 4.*

This step is the hallmark of RM, the key to bringing transparent discipline to the task of making philanthropic choices and the direct and indirect focus of the vast majority of subsequent chapters.

Recall that Step 2 says to focus on earnings and health.

Outcome 1: Boost high school graduation. Research shows that high school graduates earn about $6,500 more a year than do equivalent students who drop out—a boost worth about $100,000 if taken as an upfront lump sum payment. Research also shows that graduates live an average of 1.8 more years (in excellent health) than do equivalent students who drop out. For reasons we'll explore in chapter 3, we assign a lump sum value of $50,000 to each additional year that graduates live in good health. Thus, the health benefit can be taken to be about $90,000 per graduate ($90,000 = 1.8 × $50,000). The monetized value of Outcome 1 equals $190,000 ($100,000 + $90,000) *per graduate*. The total monetized value of Outcome 1 equals $190,000 multiplied by the number of students who graduate only because of the funder's intervention.

The point to notice is that the benefit of increasing earnings and the benefit of improving health, the objects of grant making as set out in Step 2, do not compare in any natural way. Earnings are measured in dollars. Health is measured in terms of mortality and morbidity. RM handles the problem by assigning dollar values to each benefit. Monetizing the value of dissimilar philanthropic benefits and outcomes lies at the core of RM.

Outcome 2: College persistence. The college office created under the grant works with the graduates of the middle school once they're enrolled in college so they stay enrolled and complete their course of studies. The research literature tells us that every extra year that students spend in college raises their future earnings by about $40,000 on average. The monetized value of Outcome 2 then equals about $40,000 for every student who spends an additional year in college because of the efforts of the college office.

*Step 6: Estimate the benefit/cost ratio of the intervention.*

In Step 5, we monetized the impact of an individual outcome. In Step 6, we monetize the impact an entire intervention (often a grant). *Grants can (and often do) generate multiple outcomes.*

In this case, a grant to the middle school generates two poverty-relevant outcomes. It boosts the percentage of students who graduate high school and it boosts the percentage of students who complete at least one year of college. The monetized value of the grant equals the sum of the monetized values of the distinct outcomes (correcting for double counting if possible, which is a subject discussed in chapter 3).

*The monetized value of the grant constitutes the numerator of the grant's benefit/cost ratio.* The cost of the intervention—in general, the size of the grant—constitutes the denominator. The ratio captures the overall impact of the grant per dollar of cost, a philanthropic analog to the financial rate of return on a for-profit investment.

Assume the funder makes a grant to the middle school of $290,000. Assume that the grant boosts the number of students who eventually graduate high school by 10 students. By asserting that the grant boosts the number of high school graduates by 10 we mean that 10 more students will graduate high school *than would have graduated had the grant to the middle school not been made.* (These italicized words brings to the fore the issue of counterfactual information—a topic discussed at length in chapter 4.) Finally, assume that the college service helps 25 graduates of the middle school stay enrolled in college for a year rather than suspending their college studies.

For Outcome 1: Putting all these numbers together, we estimate that for each student who graduates high school because of the grant rather than drop out, poverty fighting benefits rise by $190,000 ($100,000 earnings benefit + $90,000 health benefit). If the increase in the number of students who graduate is 10, which is the assumed impact of the grant, then the grant generates a total poverty fighting benefit of $1.9 million (10 students × $190,000 benefit/student).

For Outcome 2: Monetized value = (25 more students complete a year of college) × $40,000 higher lifetime earnings per extra year of college = $1,000,000.

Total monetized value of grant (both outcomes accounted for) = $1.9 million + $1.0 million = $2.9 million. The $2.9 million figure constitutes the numerator of the grant's benefit/cost ratio. The denominator of the benefit/cost ratio is the size of the donor's grant, or $290,000. Thus, in this hypothetical example, the estimated benefit/cost ratio is 10:1 ($2.9 million/$290,000).

How do we interpret the 10:1 estimate? The ratio says that the aggregate living standards of students at the middle school rise by $10 over their careers for each dollar the funder spends.[1]

*Step 7: Compare benefit/cost ratios for any one proposal against another.*

For the thought experiment at the top of this chapter, the philanthropist needs to compare the impact on poverty—translation, impact on earnings and health status—of spending money on job training versus spending money on improving middle school instruction. Toward that end, compare the estimates of the benefit/cost ratios for training carpenters vs. improved teaching of middle school students. Choose the intervention that delivers the most benefits per dollar. Note that for current purposes, we are assuming that estimates of benefit/cost ratios are accurate. See the embarrassing anecdote in the last section of this chapter for doses of reality.

## Thoughts About Benefit/Cost Ratios

Is the 10:1 estimate from the preceding hypothetical job training example impressively high? Disappointingly low? Answer: Neither.

First, whether 10:1 is to be treated as high or low depends first and foremost on the benefits that the funder could generate by spending its resources in some other way. In particular, whether 10:1 should be regarded as high or low depends on the benefit/cost estimate for the alternative investment, identified as carpentry training in our opening paragraph.

Here's another thought experiment. Assume that the following benefit/cost ratios are perfectly accurate (although they never will be in practice). Assume that the funder also makes a grant to a program to train unemployed women to become carpenters. Assume that this job training program generates a 4:1 benefit/cost ratio. Now ponder transferring $1 million in grants from carpentry training to the middle school. By spending $1 million less on job training, the funder can expect, at a benefit/cost ratio of 4:1, to extinguish $4 million in aggregate benefits (in the form of lower future earnings and diminished future health status of chronically unemployed women). By spending $1 million more at the middle school, the funder can expect, at a 10:1 benefit/cost ratio, to generate $10 million more in aggregate benefits. Lose $4 million. Gain $10 million. The swap of dollars to the middle school from the carpentry training generates an increase of $6 million in poverty-relevant benefits without costing the funder an extra dime.

The point? Taken at face value, benefit/cost ratios tell philanthropists how to reallocate money. Funders come out ahead by transferring money to interventions that generate high benefit/cost ratios from interventions that generate low benefit/cost ratios.[2]

We aren't trying to advocate a simplistic approach here. Smart philanthropists do not put their grant making decisions on automatic pilot. They are not slaves to simple arithmetic. In the real world, the numbers behind estimates of benefit/cost ratios do not warrant unquestioned confidence. Indeed, one of the most important uses of benefit/cost estimates is to diagnose grant proposals, not to rank them. If an intervention that excites the philanthropic imagination generates a low benefit/cost estimate when scrutinized, then the next step is to figure out why. Is the intervention weak or is the funder underestimating the impact? If, on the other hand, an intervention generates a high benefit/cost estimate, then the funder's next step is to figure out if the intervention is truly powerful or the underlying calculations exaggerate the true impact. The point is not to fudge calculations to generate a preconceived answer. Rather, the point is for practitioners of RM to learn from and react to careful readings of data. Practiced honestly and openly, RM surely beats systems that make no similar efforts to openly ground philanthropic decisions in outcomes-based numbers.

We argue that smart funders start with RM and the arithmetic it spawns. But they don't base decisions on arithmetic alone. Smart funders bring a lot more information to the task of making philanthropic decisions than simple arithmetic.

## Relentless Monetization Constitutes a Strategy

RM may look like a tactic, but in fact it's a full-blown strategy.

To appreciate the full dimension of our brand of smart philanthropy, think of a funder as a market, a market for grant proposals. The supply of grant proposals comes from lots of places: local nonprofits, national nonprofits, research results from elsewhere around the country (and world), and outcomes of local and faraway pilots.

Here's the point. Once grant making proposals appear from whatever source, the fun begins. Armed with algorithms to assign reasonable values to grants under review, no matter how different in form and purpose they might be, the funder determines their relative impact per dollar. Because RM handles all comers, it constitutes a philanthropic strategy by which to pick the right proposals to fund—"right" in the sense of generating the greatest expected benefit from the amount of money the funder makes available.

*We remind the reader that RM refers to more than arithmetic.* Yes, the arithmetic is necessary for smart diagnoses and decisions. Smart decisions won't happen without the arithmetic. But mere arithmetic is not sufficient to generate smart decisions. Funders will find that they also need to marshal qualitative information that comes by way of shrewd observation to round out their decision making processes.

We hear you muttering that RM, as described so far, cannot possibly answer strategic questions. Do we steer grants toward programs that can be scaled, or do we look just as intensively for effective programs that cannot be replicated? Do we favor programs that prevent poverty or those that cure poverty? Do we focus on innovative projects or programs that deliver reliable services? Do we prefer to serve young children over elderly adults? Do we target the neediest individuals or those with whom we can expect consistently positive results? Do we emphasize high-dose expensive programs that lift relatively few people by substantial amounts, or do we look for low-dose programs that reach huge numbers of needy individuals?

Obviously, we need to lay out answers to each such question.

Or do we?

In fact, RM, properly executed, handles each issue automatically. Take each tradeoff: replicable/nonreplicable; preventative/curative; innovative/already proved; young/old; hardest-to-serve/easiest-to-serve; high dose/low dose. Each warrants attention, but none warrants special attention. RM instructs funders to maximize mission-relevant benefits, given their budgets. Along the way, funders take explicit account of all relevant tradeoffs. No special thumb on the proverbial scale is required.

Let's consider the tradeoff between high- and low-dose interventions. High-dose interventions offer expensive treatments to relatively few participants: The idea is to deliver huge benefit to each participant. Low-dose interventions, by contrast, offer relatively inexpensive treatments to a large number of participants: The idea under this approach is that the sum total of benefits will be huge if a very large number of participants gain a modest amount. RM calculates the tradeoff correctly: For the two programs, how do the mission-relevant gains per dollar compare? RM does *not* presume to know which tactic is best in any given situation. It lets the data make that determination. So too for the other tradeoffs.

Assume two programs, AAA and BBB, help developmentally handi-capped children learn English. AAA generates fewer short-term benefits per dollar of costs than does BBB. But AAA offers better prospects for fu-ture replication (scaling). RM requires funders to tote up long-run benefits and costs; for example, taking into account the possibility that per-child costs will fall with future expansion. The approach of taking long-run pos-sibilities of expansion into account does not by itself answer which, if either, program ought to be funded. But it surely does guarantee that a short-run advantage receives no undue weight.

The strategy of RM requires funders to take explicit account of tradeoffs large and small as part of the process of estimating benefits and costs. The framework militates against deciding about tradeoffs aforethought. It calls on funders to avoid making strategic choices *before* analyzing evidence and instead, make choices *after* analyzing evidence.

## Relentless Monetization in Action: An Embarrassing Anecdote

Done correctly, RM bites hard. Take the case of Single Stop, a program cre-ated by one of the authors before he joined the staff of Robin Hood. Robin Hood now funds 80 sites across New York City to serve more than 100,000 individuals a year. (A national spinoff operates in the San Francisco Bay Area, Miami and a growing number of other cities across the country.) The staff at each site includes social workers, lawyers, and other counselors. Benefit counselors, relying on sophisticated software developed by Single Stop, link individuals to food stamps, Medicaid, federal disability pay-ments, and dozens of other city, state, and federal programs for which they qualify. Financial counselors help participants deal with debt, bankruptcy, and budgeting. Tax preparers help low-paid workers claim city, state, and federal tax refunds. Social workers and job counselors solve other prob-lems. The numbers are enormous. Last year alone, Single Stop prepared tax returns for 50,000 low-paid New Yorkers, claiming more than $100 *million* in city, state, and federal refunds on their behalf. (The $100 million figure exaggerates the impact because it takes no account of counterfactuals—how much these workers would have recovered on their own. But for now, we'll use the figure for its attention-grabbing value.)

In 2006, Robin Hood created two Single Stop sites, one for men and one for women, at Rikers Island prison, which at about 13,000 prisoners, ranks as the world's largest penal colony.

Why put a Single Stop in a prison?

Staff toted up likely poverty fighting benefits and costs. Consider the fact that about two-thirds of Rikers prisoners return to criminality within three or so years of release. Ex-offenders have little chance of surviving legally on the outside. Clearly, their chances plummet further still if they exit prison without the public props that keep the heads of other poor New Yorkers above water. Robin Hood figured it would pursue its mission by connecting prisoners to Medicaid, job counseling, lawyers, and other supports *before* they exit prison and, therefore, *before* they drown financially. That way, we'd have a chance to cut the sky-high recidivism rates and poverty that recidivism creates. In the language of RM, the size of the numerator of the benefit/cost ratio for a Single Stop site at Rikers was deemed to be potentially huge.

So Robin Hood, in partnership with the city's prison authorities, created the Rikers sites. The question then became: to what effect? To answer that question, ponder two stylized facts. First, about one-third of prisoners entering Rikers prison have been collecting government-subsidized benefits (like Medicaid and food stamps). Second, two-thirds of the prisoners who visit the Rikers Single Stop sites are enrolled in government-provided benefits programs upon exiting prison. The one-third/two-thirds contrast makes a compelling case for the proposition that the Rikers Single Stop sites are a powerhouse weapon against poverty. Case closed.

Well, not so fast—here comes the embarrassment.

Marshaling statistical evidence to pinpoint the impact of a philanthropic intervention lies at the core of RM. The process requires hard work. It does not always produce unimpeachable conclusions. But sometimes evaluators get a lucky break, known as a "natural experiment." This happened at Rikers.

The prison authorities renovated physical space for the purpose of hosting Single Stop. About two years into the Rikers Single Stop program, the roof over the site that served male prisoners began to buckle, forcing the Single Stop staff to relocate to a smaller space. All of a sudden the Rikers Single Stop, for the first time, had to turn away some of the prisoners who asked for help.

Enter the natural experiment. As practitioners of RM, Robin Hood pounced on the opportunity to create something good out of the unfortunate turn of events. It hired MDRC, a first-rate evaluator of social experiments, to randomly select which prisoners would receive the Single Stop service and which would not (given that rationing needed to be imposed, one way or another). In other words, MDRC created a randomized control trial, with a treatment and control groups, and followed the prisoners for several months after they exited Rikers.

To our dismay, MDRC found that the percentage of prisoners enrolling for government benefits in the treatment group (those who were helped by Single Stop counselors) was not much different from the percentage in the control group (those not served by Single Stop). By that cursory measure, the Rikers Single Stop site did not accomplish its mission. So much for "case closed."

How could Single Stop not work, given the fact that, as stated, twice as many Single Stop participants enroll for government benefits (two-thirds) than do incoming prisoners at large (one-third)? Answer: selection bias, a plague that runs amok through social science statistics. The prisoners who ask for Single Stop services aren't like prisoners at large. Specifically, a high proportion number of prisoners who did *not* ask for Single Stop's help apparently already knew they were ineligible for government subsidies. They knew they would be wasting their time by visiting Rikers Single Stop. And those who did choose to visit the Single Stop sites at Rikers disproportionately collected benefits even before entering prison or otherwise knew they would be eligible to receive them upon release. For them, Single Stop made enrollment for government benefits easier, but not actually more likely. Without Rikers Single Stop, they would have gotten benefits themselves.

What are the lessons for funders from the embarrassing outcome?

- Never fall in love with your own work. Even favorite children can disappoint. Let evidence prevail, embarrassment be damned.
- Take careful note of the numbers. They never ever speak for themselves. That twice as many Single Stop visitors at Rikers enroll for benefits as nonvisitors seemed surefire proof that the site was working wonders. But problems like selection bias work powerfully to make a mockery of glib inferences.
- Check for biases in evaluations, either those that exaggerate the impact of a grant or those that underestimate it. Then check again. Indeed, in this case, the MDRC evaluation was biased in the direction of underestimating the impact of the program. For starters, MDRC, by contract with Robin Hood, tracked only male ex-offenders. Let's note that female prisoners qualify for more government-subsidized benefits. Also, and again by contract with Robin Hood, MDRC tracked only enrollment in government benefit programs in its follow-up surveys. It ignored the impact of all other Single Stop services—for example, those provided by lawyers, financial counselors, and job counselors.

The MDRC Rikers study thereby systematically underestimated the true impact of the Rikers operation. Before drawing conclusions about the effectiveness of Rikers Single Stop, Robin Hood would need to conduct a far more complete study.

• Use data diagnostically. Taken at face value, the MDRC study delivers a clear direction to Robin Hood to figure out ways to draw prisoners to Single Stop who would *not* naturally visit on their own. That might sound like a Groucho Marx joke. The Rikers Single Stop site welcomes prisoners who don't want its help. In fact, the numbers gave precise direction to the Rikers sites: Find ways to attract those prisoners who don't understand the potential importance of Single Stop to their future livelihood.

• Take the time to digest evidence before taking action. Before deciding on the value of Rikers Single Stop as a poverty fighting intervention, Robin Hood needs to assign a value to all of its services, not just the impact on enrollment for government-subsidized benefits. Second, Robin Hood needs to figure out whether it can attract to its site the prisoners who truly need help. After all, there's reason for optimism. Carefully scrutinized evidence shows that Robin Hood's 60 or so other Single Stop sites work as intended. The jury remains out on Rikers (pun intended).

We present the Rikers case to emphasize the keys to practicing smart philanthropy. Collect rigorous data, seizing whatever opportunities arise. Scrutinize counterfactuals—selection bias lurks nearly everywhere. Commit to programs that demonstrate success, not those that sound nice. And, most important, use data diagnostically. Use data to identify what's not working and, perhaps, how to fix the problems. Robin Hood did not abandon Rikers. It fixed the problem by working with prison authorities to bring to Single Stop the very prisoners who most needed Robin Hood's help. These are essential lessons for any funder that chooses to practice RM.

We end this overview of RM with noteworthy observations, each discussed at length in subsequent chapters.

1. We are not the first analysts of philanthropic decisions to preach from the altar of systemization and quantification. Indeed, outcomes-based philanthropy is all the rhetorical rage these days. We say "rhetorical" because the rhetoric of accountability far outpaces actual practice. In practice, what philanthropists do indeed count is too often irrelevant or wrong. And counting wrong drives philanthropic decisions into very wrong corners. We intend to convince you that RM sets out the right ways to count. RM lays claim to handling the

problem of comparing impacts of dissimilar interventions. It lays claim to handling interventions that generate multiple benefits. And RM lays claim to handling interventions that are hard to measure and complicated to track. We address each of these claims in subsequent chapters.

2. Nor are we the first analysts of philanthropic decisions to practice benefit/cost analysis. See, for example, Paul Brest, *Money Well Spent*. Benefit/cost analysis is the mainstay of modern economic decision making and is used routinely to assess large-scale public policies (highway construction, pharmaceutical drug approval, environmental cleanup). RM takes this workhorse and applies it to the business of day-to-day philanthropy; that is to say, it applies the analytical apparatus to the type of narrow interventions that individual philanthropies routinely face. Such interventions can loom large—rewrite the curriculum of early childhood programs—lending themselves to traditional applications of benefit/cost analysis. But the type of interventions routinely funded by individual philanthropies and philanthropists can appear no larger than a pin prick: Provide showers to homeless visitors to emergency food centers. This book sets out steps for applying benefit/cost principles to hitherto overlooked circumstances.

3. RM is no milquetoast formulation; it needs to be used cautiously. It builds upon the best possible evidence. But the best available evidence can be incomplete, imprecise, and sometimes downright atrocious. In some cases, monetization reflects little more than (informed) guesswork.

For this and other reasons, prominent voices pull philanthropy in directions opposite to that of RM. George Soros, the billionaire financier and founder of the Open Society Foundations, opined in *The Chronicle of Philanthropy* that philanthropists focus too much on quantifying results. "That is a false track . . . . By insisting on measurable achievements, they very often distort the objective, and that distorts the results, too." He cited the example of the Bill & Melinda Gates Foundation and other foundations, whose fixation on vaccinating children diverted resources from overall health care and weakened some countries' health systems. Obviously, the folks at the Gates Foundation disagree, citing compelling evidence, including numbers, regarding spillovers of the infrastructure built to deliver vaccines to also fight malaria and malnutrition. Mr. Soros said his own approach is one of "trial and error."[3] But pray tell, how can a philanthropist know if his experiments have worked except by way of careful measurement of results?

In a similar vein, Mark Kramer, managing director and cofounder of FSG Social Impacts Advisors and founder of the Center for Effective

Philanthropy at Harvard University, has publicly opposed efforts to compare the value of grants that generate multiple outcomes. Indeed, Mr. Kramer has accused those of us who advocate such efforts of "setting back" the cause of effective philanthropy.[4] This book argues the contrary. Indeed, we'll argue that Mr. Kramer's widely held position is intellectually untenable.

Critics like Mr. Soros and Mr. Kramer are surely right that measuring impacts can be fiendishly difficult. They are also surely right that fixating on numbers can lead to dropping from consideration benefits that do not lend themselves to ready monetization. Here, we have a classic tradeoff. On the one hand, measurement threatens to undervalue non-pecuniary benefits. On the other hand, refusal to measure threatens to leave grant making to anecdotal whim. The reader will decide if by the end of the book we've met our burden of establishing that the importance of the second threat far outweighs that of the first. In any case, critics of measurement remind us to continuously update estimates and expand the range of benefit brought into calculations.

Peter Drucker, the acclaimed American business consultant, famously said, "What gets measured, gets done." So very true. Numerical targets tell actors (including funders and nonprofits) exactly what they need to do to succeed. Were a foundation board to instruct staff to cut street homelessness in half by year's end, then staff would know full well whether it had succeeded. No ambiguity.

There's a compelling variation on the Drucker motto: What doesn't get measured, doesn't get done. Were the foundation's board to instruct staff to reduce street homelessness, no numbers included, staff would then have broad leeway to interpret year-end results in any way that clever use of the English language allows. Unconnected to measured outcomes, the crossbar for success would, by omission, be set low. Funders would continue to spend dollars on programs whose outcomes are mediocre or worse. In a world of scarce philanthropic dollars, spending on the wrong programs equates to starving the right programs. Smart philanthropy may not sound mellow, but it is caring. Not-smart philanthropy callously wastes money, harming the families and causes that philanthropy seeks to serve.

At its core, RM is less a matter of arithmetic than of a powerful metaphor: Don't fund interventions merely because they are good. Good is not good enough. Fund interventions that, judged with the best available evidence, are the best among available options. Toward this imperative, numbers help. If handled skeptically and cautiously, numbers compel smart decisions. Okay, let's amend that sweeping statement: Numbers, if handled skeptically and cautiously, compel smart *er* decisions.

Every step along the way of RM requires debatable judgment calls. No step works magic. Each involves error. Each needs to be refined, even re-thought over time. We offer this book in the hope that the back-and-forth between us and readers will nudge the methodology along. If, at the end of the traverse, other nonprofits find something valuable to use themselves, then so much the better.

Metrics matter. Every time we err in allocating grant money—spending too much on one group and, therefore, too little on another—we leave behind needless suffering by those whom nonprofits serve. Our metrics system reflects a powerful ambition: to spend money smartly, achieving philanthropic missions as best as possible. We know that RM is not a per-fect strategy, but no other approach offers

1. philanthropic funders a better guide for allocating their money;
2. donors a better or more transparent gauge of the effectiveness of the nonprofits they make possible; or
3. nonprofits a better measure of their ability to fulfill their donor's intent.

Bon voyage.

# 2

# Translating Mission Into
# Mission-Relevant Outcomes

## Overview

In this chapter we trace the first four (of seven) steps by which philanthropist put Relentless Monetization (RM) into action.

*Step 1: Adopt a mission statement.*

An environmentalist adopts the mission of protecting the environment. A philanthropist adopts the mission of fighting poverty. A human rights activist adopts the mission of enforcing human rights.

*Step 2: Translate the mission statement into broad goals.*

The environmentalist sets the goal of saving at-risk species of plants and animals from extinction. The poverty fighter sets the goal of raising the living standards of low wage workers. And the human rights activist sets the goal of winning freedom for political prisoners in South America.

*Step 3: Identify interventions that achieve mission-driven goals.*

The environmentalist considers investing in a political campaign to block the construction of a dam across a river in Tennessee to save the threatened snail darter or creating a wildlife sanctuary to protect manatees. The poverty fighter considers investing in poorly performing urban middle schools or creating a micro-loan program for low-income women to open small businesses. The human rights activist considers efforts to lobby

Congress to shut off trade with South American countries that jail leaders of the ruling party's opposition or supporting independent journalists in a country where a free press is threatened.

*Step 4: Identify outcomes that flow from the proposed intervention and those that are relevant to the chosen mission.*

The snail darter survives, saving one species. The manatee's chances of survival improve. High school students at risk for dropping out earn their high school diplomas, thereby earning higher wages over their careers. Low-income women earn higher incomes by operating small businesses from home. South American authoritarians release political prisoners. Independent journalists in Turkmenistan get their message out.

Once these four steps are completed, the philanthropist can take on the all-important task, analyzed in the next chapter, of assigning dollar values to outcomes that flow from various actual or proposed philanthropic interventions. It is the process of monetization that enables funders to compare the value of one potential intervention against the value of any other intervention. And it is the hallmark of RM that comparisons of value are possible no matter how different the outcomes of the interventions.

Let's consider each of these steps in turn.

*Step 1: Adopt a mission statement.*

Missions vary greatly in content and specificity. We don't have much to say in this book about the origin of mission statements except to observe that they typically express a noble ambition about addressing a problem that philanthropists have come to believe is dire.

Responding to what some environmentalists perceive as alarming rates of extinction of plant and animal species, the National Fish and Wildlife Foundation supports projects that "protect and restore" endangered species. Responding to what they feared would be economic collapse following the 1987 stock market crash, the hedge fund traders who founded Robin Hood created the charity to "fight poverty in New York City." As events turned out, the ability of these hedge fund traders to predict the course of financial markets far exceeded their ability to predict the course of the economy. The nation's economy barely noticed Wall Street's 1987 collapse. But from erroneous economic forecasting came New York City's largest philanthropy dedicated solely to ameliorating poverty.

The John D. and Catherine T. McArthur Foundation builds "a more just, verdant, and peaceful world." The Rockefeller Foundation promotes "the well-being of humanity." ReServe, responding to the massive upward drift in the percentage of Americans who are, or about to be, retired, matches "professionals age 55+ with [nonprofit] organizations that need their expertise." The American Red Cross aids victims of disasters and helps people prepare for emergencies. The Center for New York City Neighborhoods "assists those at risk of losing their homes to foreclosure." The Environmental Defense Fund links "science, economics and law to create innovative, equitable and cost-effective solutions to society's most urgent environmental problems." And so on.

The point to note here is that mission statements, however unspecific, matter. They rule some interventions in. They rule other interventions out.

Imagine a grant to XYZ, a middle school in a poor urban neighborhood. The principal of XYZ boasts that her students rush home after the school bell rings to read King Lear voluntarily. Is the grant to XYZ working?

The answer depends on who's doing the judging—whose mission rules.

Take the point of view of a funder whose mission is to deepen knowledge and respect of Western culture. For this funder, XYZ works fantastically well. But, take the point of view of a nonprofit dedicated to ameliorating poverty and you may well get a different judgment. The nonprofit would measure success not by the number of students who read Shakespeare, but by the number of high school students a school graduates on time. (Research shows that there's simply no better ticket out of poverty than a high school diploma.) Like the culture lover, poverty-fighting nonprofits value literacy. But for those focused on poverty-fighting, reading Ian Fleming (the trials and tribulations of superspy James Bond) is not obviously inferior to reading Shakespeare's *Hamlet* (the trials and tribulations of an anguished Danish prince). If the Shakespeare readers drop out of high school in no fewer numbers than James Bond readers, funders focused on poverty fighting would find nothing exciting about the program.

One school. Two funders. Two missions. Two measures of success. Two (different) judgments.

Our little example has several implications.

First, a nonprofit's mission dictates what it will count toward success. A nonprofit needs to think deeply about its mission statement because, as we've just seen, its definition of mission will determine which initiatives it will or will not fund. And because defining mission is so critical, the process of crafting the mission statement is bound to be an iterative one.

Second, nonprofits and their funders need to achieve the proper generality. Defining a mission too narrowly risks turning off an excessive number of potential donors. The Einhorn Family Foundation focuses on teaching tolerance to schoolchildren. As a family funded foundation, it has the luxury of proceeding without need to attract nonfamily donors. If, by contrast, a charity were to focus on bullying, it might find too few donors (whatever one's view of the merits of the programmatic focus). Overly narrow missions create another problem: inflexibility. An after-school program dedicated to teaching youngsters how to use a slide rule would have made sense in the 1960s but not thereafter.

For a nonprofit to make the opposite mistake—defining its mission too broadly—risks exciting no group of potential donors in particular. A nonprofit that declares its goal is to improve the character of schoolchildren might well leave potential donors mystified by what the nonprofit truly intends to do with its donors' money and concerned about its ability to properly allocate resources in pursuit of such an ill-defined goal.

The latter concern is well founded. The central argument of this book is that effectively measuring success is the sine qua non of smart philanthropy; however, mission and measurement are inextricably linked: Each plays a critical role in defining the other.

A system of metrics—the tools and procedures by which to measure a nonprofit's success—starts with the nonprofit's mission statement. Robin Hood's mission is to "fight poverty." The mission statements of most nonprofits sound similarly inspirational. Examples: training children for twenty-first century jobs; closing the academic achievement gap between haves and have nots; or giving victims of domestic violence a safe haven. The "metrics" (the measure of success) of the one will not be appropriate for the others.

This seemingly elementary declaration is not as obvious as it might sound. Take poverty-relevant interventions that have environmental consequences. For example, a program that trains unemployed workers to become environmentally sensitive ("green") carpenters produces two outcomes. First, the training boosts the future income of the newly credentialed carpenters. Second, it improves the environment. But when Robin Hood measures the impact of its grants, it counts the value of environmental gains as zero. To do otherwise would steer Robin Hood's money in the wrong direction, in a direction dictated neither by its mission nor its donors. Robin Hood should no more count environment-related outcomes of its grants than the Environmental Defense Fund should count literacy gains among those who clean the environment. If the reader is tempted to say, why not have all the nonprofits count all socially valuable outcomes when they measure success, and in this way have "shared metrics," resist the temptation. Sharing metrics might sound akin to preaching brotherly love, but in this case sharing is not caring. Because metrics are defined by mission, the only way to have fully shared metrics is for all nonprofits to have the same, extremely vague, mission, which is the same as all nonprofits having no specific mission at all. Any such dilution of nonprofits' mission would spray money in directions that their donors did not intend (and would not long tolerate). No less a problem, nonprofits having no clear mission would make monitoring the effectiveness of their programs much more difficult, both from within and without.

We've been arguing that mission defines metrics. But we've also said that metrics play a critical role in defining mission. How and why? Smart philanthropy is all about spending money well. If a nonprofit's mission defies measurement, then the nonprofit will spend money unwisely, and this waste is exactly what smart philanthropy sets out to avoid. A nonprofit's first draft of its mission generates implicit metrics by which to measure success. But if upon reflection those metrics look like they will be unworkably complicated, vague, or inaccurate, then the nonprofit's next course of action is to rework its mission. Defining a mission becomes an iterative process. For a nonprofit to succeed in its mission, it needs workable metrics to guide its decisions. However inspiring a mission statement, a nonprofit that proceeds without a consistent set of metrics by which to judge its impact is virtually guaranteeing failure.

*Step 2. Translate mission statement into well-defined goals.*

As a rule, mission statements play better as inspirational oratory than as guides to action. To determine if mission and metrics are mutually compatible, the funder must translate its mission into well-defined goals. These goals, in turn, serve as clear benchmarks by which to judge the nonprofit's success, the basis for its metrics. An important point to make here is that goals must be practical. They must work as useful guidelines for action.

As one example, let's trace the details by which Robin Hood has translated its mission of fighting poverty into actionable goals.

Robin Hood has chosen to translate the mission of fighting poverty into the goal of raising the living standard of poor New Yorkers. That translation might seem to the reader as little more than a move from one stock phrase (fighting poverty) to another (raising living standards). But in fact, this innocuous sounding translation drives grant making in decisive and even controversial directions. Here are three examples.

First, the translation focuses on changes rather than levels. Robin Hood aims to raise—that is to say, change—the living standards of poor New Yorkers. Robin Hood could have chosen differently; for example, by setting its goal in terms of a particular level of well-being. For example, Robin Hood could have defined its goals as lifting the most New Yorkers above the federal government's office poverty threshold (in 2012, about $23,000 of income a year for a family of four). Had Robin Hood done so, the pattern of its grant making would be radically different. Why? Because resources would have flowed to initiatives targeted at those whose income was just a tad below the poverty threshold rather than those who were further from that threshold.

Second, "living standards" is a purposely elastic term, allowing for implementation to evolve over time. As of now, Robin Hood measures two features of living standards: income and health status. If a grant lifts the future earnings of low-income New Yorkers, Robin Hood counts the impact as poverty fighting. And if a grant makes poor New Yorkers healthier, we count the impact as poverty fighting.

Third, living standards, in most applications of the term, does not include feelings of physical or emotional safety. Robin Hood, at least so far, counts neither. Here, too, Robin Hood might well have decided otherwise. Consider George Soros, the multi-billionaire philanthropist. When he made a grant of $125 million to create after-school programs in New York City public schools, he did not (as confirmed during a private conversation with one of the authors) primarily intend to improve student test scores. Instead, he wanted poor families to have the peace of mind that their children were in a safe, constructive place once the school bell rang in the afternoon. When Robin Hood partnered with Mr. Soros's foundation to expand after-school options in New York City, it did not count as one of the initiative's mission-relevant outcomes the safety that parents felt by enrolling their children. Robin Hood estimated by how much the after-school sites raised academic performance (and, therefore, how much the sites raised the odds that the children would eventually graduate high school). This is another example of one program, two missions and, therefore, different metrics.

Mr. Soros's after-school programs would have looked a lot more attractive to Robin Hood had the latter factored in parental perceptions of safety as part of its definition of living standards. That raises the question, is Robin Hood's prism too narrow? Perhaps. But Robin Hood chooses to use its more narrow measure of living standards, and therefore a more narrow measure of success—that is, improvements in poor New Yorkers' living standards–for a good reason: At present it does not have a good way to measure, much less place a value on, parental perceptions of safety. If Robin Hood were to broaden its mission to include parental perceptions of safety, it would have no good way to gauge its success in fulfilling the (widened) mission. The measurement problem is not insurmountable. Social scientists are at work trying to craft good measures of physical insecurity.

Here is a vivid example of our point about the iterative nature of choosing missions and metrics. Without a measure of physical insecurity, Robin Hood has no good way to amend its mission-driven goal to improve the living standards of poor New Yorkers to incorporate perceptions of safety. But were Robin Hood to craft or find a reliable measure of insecurity, then it could revise its goals accordingly. It would have what it needs to measure success.

Over the next couple of years, Robin Hood will review what it has come to mean by living standards. It might, as discussed, add perceptions of safety. It might add other variables. The United Kingdom and other Western European industrialized countries have incorporated some specific components of material deprivation into their concepts of living standards; for example, the United Kingdom tracks the lack of access to cell phones or the Internet when gauging changes in living standards. Robin Hood might decide to follow suit.[1]

The point to note here is that because Robin Hood has chosen a somewhat elastic term—living standards—by which to define its mission-driven goal, it can expand or shrink its working definitions without amending basic documents or organizational purpose. As metrics emerge to track subtle components of well-being, they can be added to the working definition of living standards without undergoing a wrenching process of revisiting the charity's basic poverty-fighting mission. What might have seemed like a flaw—an elastic translation of "poverty fighting" into "living standards"—turns out to be a virtue.

*Step 3: Identify interventions.*

In Step 3, the philanthropist identifies plausible interventions to achieve mission-relevant goals.

Robin Hood employs dozens of different interventions to fight poverty. Among them: microloans to immigrant entrepreneurs; charter schools at the elementary, middle, and high school levels; job training for female commercial truck drivers; lawyers for ex-offenders to counter eviction notices; shelters for victims of domestic violence; anti-obesity programs for elementary school students; soup kitchens; academically focused prekindergarten programs. We make the important point here, to be developed later in the book, that funders need not be constrained in terms of the approach by which they identify plausible interventions. They can emerge from musings or practices of academics, legislators, policymakers, philanthropists, or nonprofit staffs. They can rain down on the philanthropic sector like proverbial manna from heaven.

Indeed, for many purposes funders might view themselves as a farmer's market. But in this case, the market is not stuffed with vendors selling fruits and vegetables. Rather, it is stuffed with nonprofits selling ideas for philanthropic interventions. In the commercial world, the goods that sell in a market are sorted and ranked by the interaction of demand and supply. In the philanthropic world, by contrast, competition cannot be relied upon to select for the good interventions and drive out the bad interventions. The task of sorting and ranking is left to the funder. The question is how the funder should proceed to do so. Funders' basic problem has been the lack of a "natural" way to compare the relative mission-relevant impact of different types of interventions—to compare the impact of a soup kitchen to that of a microloan. Our view is that RM provides a neat way to sort, analyze and, yes, rank potential interventions.

### Step 4: Identify mission-relevant outcomes.

This step calls on funders to identify the mission-relevant outcomes that might flow from potential interventions. In general, interventions (grants) trigger multiple outcomes. For a funder focused on Third World economic development, building a centrally located tube well can affect rural villages not only by reducing deaths from water-borne illnesses, but also by making it possible for young women to attend school because they no longer need to haul water from distant springs or wells. Similarly, a grant to an urban high school to improve the future financial fortunes of students may not only raise on-time graduation rates, but also raise college enrollment as a second outcome.

As was true of Step 3 (identifying interventions), there is no single procedure by which to generate a list of mission-relevant outcomes that flow from each different intervention. A list of outcomes typically emerges from the usual suspects: academics, philanthropists, nonprofits, government officials, and think tanks. What's important is not the source of a list of potential outcomes, but how the funder makes use of a list, whatever its source. Ultimately, the funder needs a way to compare the importance of different types of outcomes. RM provides just such a way, as we show in the next chapter, by assigning monetary value to any such outcomes.

Let's mull three examples.

### Example 1

Our first example highlights how mission defines what counts as a mission-relevant outcome.

Take a grant by Robin Hood to a charter high school. To proceed, we need take account of Robin Hood's specific mission, poverty fighting. And we need to take account of Robin Hood's broad goals, raising living standards. The question is how the grant might contribute to furthering Robin Hood's mission.

Social science research identifies a decisive answer. A grant to a charter high school can reduce poverty, as we've pointed out before, if it raises the number of students who graduate rather than drop out. Each additional graduate can be expected to earn more income and enjoy better health over his or her lifetime compared with demographically similar high school students who drop out short of graduation.

Now change the mission. Suppose that instead of fighting poverty, the funder makes a grant to a charter high school to increase the supply of world-class scientists. With that mission, the number of graduates is not a mission-relevant outcome. Graduating academically marginal students matters naught. The funder of a charter high school with a superstar scientist mission would fixate instead on increasing only the number of superstar graduates.

To drive home the point, suppose that the grant to the charter school not only increases the graduation rate of marginal students, but also increases the number of gifted students who become science superstars. How would Robin Hood assess the grant? For Robin Hood, the number of gifted students who vault into superstar status does not matter because they were never in danger of dropping out or winding up poor. Producing more science superstars might be a nice sounding outcome from a number of perspectives, but they are not a mission-relevant outcome to Robin Hood. The outcome that matters comes from increasing the graduation rates of students at risk for dropping out. As we've said, mission governs all.

*Example 2*

Our second example points to interventions that yield multiple (mission-relevant) outcomes.

Consider a funder that makes a grant to a nonprofit that trains unemployed women to become entry level carpenters. Suppose, to complicate matters, the nonprofit also enrolls its trainees in government subsidized programs like food stamps, Medicaid (health insurance), and day care. Suppose, further, that the nonprofit connects its trainees to free financial counselors (primarily to deal with debt) and free tax preparers (primarily for the purpose of applying for tax refunds on behalf of workers who earn low wages). Finally, suppose that the nonprofit links trainees to subsidized medical clinics and lawyers to represent the trainees on civil matters like disputes over child custody. In short, this is a classic example of a single grant producing many different mission-relevant outcomes.

To a funder whose mission is to fight poverty, what mission-relevant outcomes flow from this grant? An initial list would include:

- Higher earnings from working as a trained carpenter;
- Higher earnings because subsidized day care allows parents to work more hours;
- Higher income resulting from tax refunds that accrue to workers with low wages;
- Improved health status because of medical insurance;
- Free legal representation for parents in civil disputes regarding custody of their children;
- Lower debt and higher credit scores because of smarter financial decisions.

We'll deal in the next chapter with the challenge of assigning value to these different outcomes, including intangible outcomes such as providing legal representation to litigants in civil matters so they get their day in court.

*Example 3*

Take a grant by a poverty-fighting funder to a soup kitchen that provides free emergency food to poor urban residents. (Soup kitchens serve hot food to poor individuals.) The funder might well go beyond covering the cost of providing hot meals. Taking advantage of the fact that soup kitchens attract very poor individuals, the funder can provide money for the soup kitchen to screen visitors for eligibility for public and private anti-poverty programs. For example, the funder's grant might require the soup kitchen to connect eligible visitors to federal food subsidies (previously called food stamps and now called Supplemental Nutrition Assistance Program, or SNAP), health insurance (Medicaid), and government subsidized job-training programs. If so, here are several mission-relevant outcomes that the grant might generate:

- Free food allows the family to spend more of its limited dollars on goods other than food. In effect, free food increases the family's income.
- Enrollees in food stamps, like recipients of free food, can spend more of their limited income on goods other than food—in effect, as before, an increase in family income.

- Free food improves the family's nutritional intake, leading to improved health status.
- Visitors enroll in government subsidized health insurance (e.g., Medicaid), cutting their outlays on health care and thereby allowing the families to spend more of their limited dollars for other purposes. As with free food, free health insurance increases the family's income.
- Medicaid coverage improves the family's health status. This impact is distinct from that of coverage on spendable income.
- Visitors receive financial counseling, thereby stanching the loss of wealth that comes with postponed bankruptcy and helping the family avoid bad decisions regarding savings, borrowing, insurance, and the like.

The question arises whether the listed nutrition outcome is truly additive to the income effect from free or subsidized food. Asked another way, does the third bullet point belong, given the first two?

In part, the answer to this question reduces to a simpler question: Should the funder be willing to pay more per meal to an emergency food program that spends money to provide extra nutritious food? The answer depends on the funder's mission. Consider Soup Kitchen A and Soup Kitchen B. Soup Kitchen A provides free meals with no special effort to make them nutritious. Soup Kitchen B provides exactly as many meals as does Soup Kitchen A but, unlike Soup Kitchen A, spends extra money to ensure that its meals are nutritionally balanced. Enter mission. A funder that's concerned with the living standard of visitors to soup kitchens would be willing, at least in theory, to give a larger grant to Soup Kitchen B than Soup Kitchen A, thereby giving incentive to soup kitchens to look after the medical well-being of their visitors. How much more per meal would a funder be willing to pay Soup Kitchen B? We answer that question in the next chapter.

## What *Not* to Fund

Let's trace the implication of identifying outcomes according to a funder's mission by focusing on outcomes that should *not* be counted.

Take a grant to a community-based organization that provides mentors to adolescent ex-offenders for the purpose of reducing recidivism. What interventions should the funder pay for?

Let's focus on two categories of possible outcomes.

First, there are outcomes that accrue to individuals. Take mentoring of at-risk youth. If successful, mentoring might help youth avoid criminal activity, avoid jail, enjoy higher paid work, and live longer, healthier lives. Robin Hood counts all of these.

Second, there are outcomes that accrue to the general population, typically non-poor taxpayers. If mentoring cuts criminality and incarceration, then a grant to provide mentors to at-risk youth will reduce the need for taxpayers to build and run prisons. Here's the odd implication of RM. Robin Hood counts the outcome of cutting expenditures on prisons as zero—zero—because the lion's share of the tax savings accrues to non-poor individuals. Donors give Robin Hood money to help poor New Yorkers. They do not give Robin Hood money to give the typical taxpayer a tax cut. The counting of some outcomes but not others dramatically affects what Robin Hood chooses to fund or not fund.

If ignoring important societal outcomes like taxpayer savings seems wrongheaded, consider the implication were Robin Hood to take taxpayer into account. Robin Hood would be left to steer its money to a wide variety of interventions that help the general (that is to say, non-poor) taxpayer, from scientific research to policy campaigns that aim to change zoning laws. The problem is that, however generally worthy these interventions might be, they would wrongly steer donor money far afield from fighting poverty.

Our point is not to urge nonprofits to steer clear of outcomes for the general population. Instead, we point to the need to match outcomes with mission. Some missions compel funders to hunt for outcomes that accrue to the general population. Other missions compel funders to hunt for outcomes for subpopulations or other narrowly defined targets. The process of deciding which potential outcomes *not* to count is every bit as important as deciding which outcomes to count.

Let's note that some of Robin Hood's biggest donors are also major benefactors of the environmental movement around the world. Yet Robin Hood's metrics ignore environmental gains. That's perfectly fine. Having the same person direct donations to different nonprofits, each with a clear mission—in this case, poverty fighting and environmental protection, respectively—almost surely will achieve both philanthropic goals better than everyone donating to all-purpose, do-good philanthropies that have no clear purpose and no clear criteria for spending their money. A diffuse mission diffuses accountability.[2]

The key point? The care with which nonprofits identify mission-relevant outcomes of proposed grants matters hugely. When a nonprofit is evaluating an initiative for funding, it should first identify all the significant mission-relevant outcomes that might flow from funding the initiative. Then it should vet the list to be sure that it includes *only* those that are relevant to the mission. The distinction between individual and social benefits might not have caught your eye upon first reading Robin Hood's translation of its mission into concrete goals, but the distinction exists and carries muscular implications.

Let's conclude this discussion with an example of an actual church-based philanthropy in New York City. For this purpose, let's call it Giving is Beautiful. Its top officials asked one of the authors for suggestions about metrics. As the conversation evolved, it became clear that Giving is Beautiful's philanthropic purpose is diametrically opposite that of Robin Hood. Robin Hood bases grants *solely* according to their expected impact on the intended recipients of its philanthropy, the poor residents of New York City. Giving is Beautiful does nearly the opposite. Its staff bases grants according to the expected impact on the donors (rather than the recipients). For example, Giving is Beautiful often prefers activities that involve volunteering, even if the volunteer activities are of little value to the recipients. To the elders of the church, engagement of one's time packs a more profound wallop than does a simple gift of cash.

The point here is not that philanthropic activities are good or bad, right or wrong. Philanthropic outcomes can be judged only by reference to mission. Robin Hood organizes volunteer efforts if they deliver high-impact services to the poor. By contrast, Giving is Beautiful views the impact of volunteering on volunteers as the object of its church-related mission. The two nonprofits pursue radically different missions and, therefore, make radically different decisions.

The inquiring reader might well ask, would Robin Hood fund an effort to organize low-impact volunteering if doing so might stimulate volunteers to become more generous donors? The answer is yes. But let's not lose sight of the distinction. The mission of Giving is Beautiful drives it to organize low-impact (from Robin Hood's perspective) volunteering and, yes, low-impact donations, because the donor comes away well served, as seen from the vantage point of the church. Robin Hood would engage in low-impact volunteering only as the means to a different end—a way to generate cash donations to Robin Hood that could then be translated into high-impact donations on behalf of New York's poor. Different missions mean different decisions regarding what counts as a mission-relevant outcome. That, in turn, will mean different decisions about which proposals to fund. For now, that's an all-important point.

# 3

# Basics of Monetizing Outcomes

This chapter examines in more detail the principles behind monetizing individual outcomes, the analytical springboard for our concept of smart philanthropy. In subsequent chapters, we take up the challenges posed by estimating counterfactual outcomes (those that would have occurred even without the help of the funder), discounting (the balancing of future vs. immediate outcomes) and monetizing entire grants, which, as flagged in chapter 1, we treat as a combination of outcomes.

We write these chapters from the point of view of a funder. But the analysis would be the same were this chapter written from the vantage point of nonprofits, policy makers, or any other party that spends money to achieve philanthropic goals.[1]

## Monetizing Distinct Outcomes

Funders virtually always have a choice of outcomes that could serve to advance their mission. Therefore, to know which initiatives to fund so as to best achieve that mission, RM calls for monetizing each distinct outcome. For example, in the case of a funder whose mission is to ameliorate poverty, those outcomes might include helping (1) chronically unemployed women find work in the construction industry; (2) at-risk students complete high school and enroll in two-year colleges; (3) immigrant women start hair-cutting operations in their home basements; (4) financially illiterate parents prepare budgets with the help of disinterested financial counselors; and (5) abused women get orders of protection against abusive husbands. Clearly, it is harder to place a value of some of the outcomes than others.

The basic idea behind monetizing these outcomes is to identify the links between these outcomes and the goals the funder has included within its measure of success (see chapter 2). Funders, in general, identify more than one goal. Therefore, the value attached to achieving a particular outcome requires quantifying the extent to which achieving that outcome advances each of the funder's goals. Then comes aggregation. The total value of the outcome equals the sum of the contributions of that outcome toward achieving each goal (issues of correcting for double counting aside).

## Monetizing High School Graduation

To make matters concrete, let's imagine a grant by a poverty-fighting funder to help high school dropouts re-enroll and earn their diplomas.

First, the funder needs to tie the outcome (graduation) to its basic goals. Let's assume, as is true of Robin Hood, that these two goals are raising income and improving health. This step forces us to confront a fundamental problem of assessment. The high school intervention generates two dissimilar benefits, and the dissimilar benefits are measured in dissimilar units. Changes in future earnings are measured in dollars, but changes in future health status are measured by changes in mortality and morbidity. Estimating the aggregate impact of high school interventions requires creating a common yardstick for the two benefits, and the only practical common yardstick is the dollar.

### MONETIZING INCOME BOOST

Research tells us that the graduates will earn an average of $6,500 a year more than dropouts with similar demographic characteristics. Over the course of a career, say 20 years, those annual $6,500 payments will add up to a large amount for each graduate. It might be tempting to calculate that large amount by simply multiplying the $6,500 per year by the number of years remaining in the graduate's working life. But to do that would be to ignore the fact that some of those benefits will be coming many years in the future, and that, as a practical matter, we don't place the same value on benefits that accrue in the future as we do on those that arrive sooner; instead, we discount them, and the further in the future they accrue, the more we discount them. (How many funders would be indifferent between an intervention that yields $100,000 of benefits this year and one that also yields $100,000 of benefits, but not until 25 years have passed?) In chapter 5 we provide a more complete explanation of how to calculate the discounted value (referred to as the "present discounted value") of a stream of annual benefits; but suppose for now that we assess the discounted value of that stream of $6,500 annual income improvements to be about $100,000.

The second benefit from graduating high school involves health. High school graduates enjoy longer, healthier lives than do demographically similar dropouts, and this health boost is a result of reasons other than the fact that graduates earn more money. The medical economics literature estimates that graduates live on average an extra 1.8 years in good health. Taking stock, we know that someone who graduates from high school as a result of the intervention (that is, someone who would have dropped out without the funder's intervention) would earn about $120,000 more over the career and live an additional 1.8 years in good health. But how should we aggregate the value of those two benefits? Clearly, the funder needs to monetize the 1.8 years of additional life into a dollar figure that can be added to the $100,000. Toward that end, we need to take a detour into the medical economics literature.

## MONETIZING HEALTH BOOST: THE ISSUE OF QUALITY-ADJUSTED LIFE YEARS

To monetize changes in health status, Robin Hood borrows from medical economics researchers a measure called a QALY (quality-adjusted life year). Developed over the past three decades, a QALY captures the impact of interventions on mortality and morbidity. It is now used extensively throughout the public policy literature.

Specifically, a QALY measures the change brought on by a health-related intervention in both the number of years an individual can be expected to live and the change in health status over the course of the individual's lifetime. In effect, each year of an individual's life is assigned a QALY *weight* that reflects the quality of his or her health during the year. The QALY weight reflects how closely the individual's medical well-being approximates perfect health. An intervention that increases an individual's longevity by an average of one year at perfect health is assigned a QALY of 1.0. An intervention that increases an individual's longevity by an average of one year but only at half-perfect health is assigned a QALY of 0.5. And an intervention that does not increase longevity at all, but increases the quality of an individual's health this year from half-perfect to perfect is also assigned a QALY of 0.5. Thus, a vaccine that extends the life of patients by an average of four years at full health is assigned a QALY value of 4.0 per patient. Were the vaccine instead to extend the life of patients by an average of six years, but the patients live those extra years at only one-half full health, then the QALY value would drop to 3.0 per patient.

There are two questions. First, how do researchers determine the expected impact of an intervention on morbidity and mortality? Second, how do researchers translate any particular configuration of physical or mental conditions into QALY weights; that is, what conditions constitute full health, two-thirds full health, half full health and other percentages of full health? Delving deeply into either question would take us far beyond the confines of this book. The important point is that serious, peer-reviewed literature has developed a methodology to answer these two questions. The argument of this book is not that QALY as a concept or the QALY values used by any particular researcher provide an indisputable way to capture the impact of medical programs. Experts continue to debate the accuracy and fairness of QALY values despite their extensive use. Our argument is simpler. QALY values provide plausible measures of health improvements, although plausible does not mean indisputable.[2]

So what does the literature tell us about the impact of high school graduation on health? Here, Robin Hood commissioned outside experts to estimate the impact of its health-related grants. Any funder applying RM will want to consider doing the same: tapping academic and other outside experts. Robin Hood repeatedly commissions studies by outsiders of the impact of its grants, including studies that have evaluated Robin Hood's education and job training grants.

In the case at hand, Robin Hood reached out to one of the country's leading experts on medical economics, Professor Peter Muennig of Columbia University. Professor Muennig was asked to estimate the impact of every Robin Hood grant that had the potential to affect the future health status of participants. Said another way, he was asked to estimate QALY values for each health-related grant. The previously cited figure of 1.8—the estimate that high school graduates live nearly two years longer at full health than do otherwise similar students who drop out—came from Prof. Muennig's report.

Now comes the tricky step: Monetizing QALYs.

Robin Hood needs to measure changes in health status in the same units that it measures changes in income: the dollar. The conversion is anything but straightforward. To give a flavor of the gnarly complications, let's trace some of Robin Hood's journey.

### Is $100,000 per Quality-Adjusted Life Year Right?

Robin Hood looked first to the way that public authorities monetized health impact of public sector investments like highway construction. When they decide whether to widen a highway to make it safer, they compare the cost of widening the highway to the collective value of saving lives and avoiding injuries. The averted deaths and injuries are measured in QALYs. The agencies then face Robin Hood's problem. How should QALYs be converted into dollars? One often-used value is $100,000 per QALY.

However, for reasons discussed below, Robin Hood's staff has decided that $100,000 is too high, threatening to steer Robin Hood grant making in unfortunate directions.

Compare two ways that a funder can assist poor, unemployed women. Assume that the two programs cost exactly the same amount, and that the funder must choose either of two options but not both or a mixture of both.

• Option #1: a job training program that will raise average annual incomes of participants to $15,000 from $6,000. That's an income boost of $9,000 a year. Let's assume that the income boost lasts 25 years (unrealistically long, but useful for exposition), for a present discounted value of about $160,000.

• Option #2: a screening center that will test low income families for colon cancer. Assume that the screening extends longevity by an average of 2.8 years in perfect health (unrealistic, but useful for exposition). At $100,000 per QALY, the medical intervention would be assigned a value of $280,000.

At first glance, the health program outperforms the job training ($280,000 vs. $160,000). But it's been Robin Hood's experience that poor parents, for compelling reasons, prefer programs that put food on their family's table today to programs that might tack on an extra year or two to their lives at some distant point in the future.

Consider two points. First, funders are justifiably uncomfortable steering participants to programs that they resist. Second, converting QALYs into dollars, a value judgment, packs profound consequences. The funder can pay to help unemployed workers find jobs, or it can pay to help screen poor people for colon cancer and other illnesses. But because resources are limited, it cannot generally do both. So what's the right choice? The choice for the dollar equivalent of a QALY steers that decision in no small part. For the outlined options, at about $100,000 per QALY, medical interventions win. Below about $50,000 per QALY, jobs programs win.

What number has Robin Hood assigned? Staff took note of the literature on international development, some of which sets the value of a QALY equal to a country's income per capita. That suggests a QALY value far below $100,000; indeed, perhaps as low as $20,000 or even less for low income neighborhoods in New York City. But a key piece of evidence comes from the United Kingdom's official panel for estimating the numerical value of medical interventions. The National Institute for Health and Clinic Excellence (NICE), part of the United Kingdom's National Health Service, has rejected payment in recent years for interventions that cost more than about $47,000 per QALY per year.[3]

Robin Hood deemed the NICE figure appropriate given the absence of a single official value in the United States and the not wildly dissimilar demographics between many patients served by the National Health Service and low income New Yorkers.

Robin Hood has settled on $50,000 per QALY, a crude resolution of uncertain tradeoffs. Setting the QALY value high (say $100,000) harms Bedford Stuyvesant residents by denying them nonmedical programs they crave. Setting the value low (say $10,000) would deny the residents important medical improvements. Like so much else described in this book, the choice comes down to a judgment call that's informed by, but not precisely determined by, research.

Judgment. Judgment. Judgment. There's simply no getting around judgment. But judgment that is informed by relentless monetization has a far better chance of being good judgment. Neither Robin Hood nor any other funder can prove that its figure for the value of a QALY is right, whatever right might mean in this context. But what funders can do is use figures that are reasonable and fit well within the boundaries of expert opinion. And funders can make those figures explicit, which has several important advantages. First, attaching dollar figures to intangible, difficult-to-measure, benefits such as QALYs allows nonprofits to see clearly the role those figures play in funding decisions. They can then adjust those figures when they seem to steer resources in ways that seem to defy good sense. Second, explicit figures for the intangibles let important sunshine into what might otherwise be a black box decision process. Explicit figures make it possible for interested parties—donors, employees, outside experts—to take a critical look and decide for themselves whether they like what the funder has done. Critics are free to substitute their own figures and reach whatever conclusions they wish. By making metrics explicit, funders can invite debate and revision.

Robin Hood's own experience with placing a value on a QALY provides an example of the process at work. When Robin Hood called on Prof. Muennig and his research colleagues to provide advice, their primary task was to estimate the impact on health—the impact on QALYs—of Robin Hood's health-related grants. They were not asked to assign a dollar value of those impacts. The figure of $100,000 per QALY that *monetized* those impacts was a figure sometimes used in benefit/cost calculations by federal agencies. When one of the authors of this book looked at what that $100,000 figure implied for the monetized values of some of RH's health-related interventions, he found figures that seemed far too large. Specifically, the monetized value of health gains appeared out of whack relative to the income boost that Robin Hood had estimated for its grants. The danger was that Robin Hood's funding decisions, assuming health gains would be measured at $100,000 per QALY, would be biased toward health-related interventions and therefore away from income improving interventions.

At his suggestion, Robin Hood undertook the exercise of recalculating the estimated value of its grants using different (lower) values of a QALY to answer two questions. Did the $100,000 figure make a significant difference in the benefit-per-dollar ranking of Robin Hood's grants? And did changes in the figure seem to produce more sensible measures of the benefits from those grants? The answer to both questions was determined to be yes. Robin Hood has since set the monetized value of a QALY at $50,000 and allocated grants accordingly. This kind of debate and revision would have been difficult, probably impossible, in the absence of the transparency that an explicit dollar figure for QALYs provides.

In an environment in which judgment calls are unavoidable, the transparency provided by clear and explicit metrics contributes in important ways to smart philanthropy and the ongoing effort to make it ever smarter.

With a decision about the dollar value of QALY in tow, let's return to our high school grant. Based on the previously cited estimate that high school graduates outlive otherwise identical high school dropouts by the equivalent of 1.8 years at perfect health, Robin Hood estimates that high school graduation generates $90,000 (1.8 QALYs × $50,000/QALY) in health benefits per graduate. Add in the earnings boost of $100,000 per graduate, the total poverty-fighting value per graduate equals $190,000, of which $100,000 reflects higher earnings and $90,000 reflects better health.

## Aggregation

So far, we've determined that the impact of the grant per graduate is $190,000 (present discounted value). Now we need to estimate the total impact of the grant. Let's assume that as a result of the grant a funder makes to a high school, 30 students graduate who would otherwise have dropped out. Then the grant causes the collective living standards of poor New Yorkers to rise by a total of $5.7 million ($190,000 × 30 graduates). Of the $5.7 million, $3 million comes in the form of higher earnings and $2.7 million comes in the form of better health. With the $5.7 million estimate in hand, the funder can now compare the total poverty-fighting benefits generated by this grant to the total poverty-fighting benefits generated by other grants (whether to high schools or other types of community-based organizations). (Chapter 8 stitches together estimates of benefits with estimates of costs to derive benefit/cost ratios.)

It is this type of methodical outcome-by-outcome monetization that justifies the name for our concept of smart philanthropy, Relentless Monetization. As examples in later chapters show, typical grants generate multiple benefits and, therefore, complicated computations. Based on nothing more than this glimpse of what's to come, let's take stock of what's gained from this benefit-by-benefit monetization:

- Funders can use the procedure to make reasonable, and defensible, decisions about the best grantees *of a given type* to back. Here, for example, the funder picks the best schools to fund, comparing any one school against another.
- Funders can use the procedure to compare the impact of grants to high schools to the impact of grants to *other types* of mission-relevant nonprofits—comparing the impact of a charter high school to the impact of, say, a program that trains unemployed women to set up day care operations in their homes.

- Because the arithmetic by which the monetized values are derived can (and, we argue, should) be made explicit, interested parties (donors, funders, nonprofits, or anyone else) can see how the numbers would change as new information appears (for example, new research on the impact of high school graduation on future earnings) or as an interested party substitutes its own numerical weights on outcomes for those used by any particular funder.

### The Threat of Double Counting

In the previous example, we derived the total value created by a grant to charter high schools by adding the values assigned to each of the two benefits involved (income and health). Simple addition is justified in this one example because the research literature on the subject provides careful evidence that the health benefit is separate from and in addition to the earnings benefit. However, in many situations, there exists no reliable basis for such simple addition.

Take XYZ, which serves troubled children by providing several services: shelters for abandoned children; nurseries for at-risk newborns; foster care and adoption services; and medical programs for young children. A funder whose mission is to ameliorate poverty might itemize the following benefits: participating children engage in less crime, receive better parenting, live longer, and enjoy better mental health; poor neighbors of participating children suffer from fewer criminal acts. Under ideal circumstances, research would provide studies that simultaneously estimate the value of these separate benefits, distinguishing each from the others. But in fact, funders are almost always faced with relying on separate studies, each focusing on a different benefit without reference to others.

Assume, for example, that the funder locates a respected study that estimates the impact of mental health counseling on recidivism. Assume that another respected study estimates the impact of mentoring on recidivism. The funder cannot be sure that a grant that provides both mental health counseling and mentoring will cut recidivism by the sum of the two individual studies. The true aggregate impact might be larger than the sum of the separate parts because the two interventions (mentoring and mental health counseling) accentuate each other. Also possible, the two interventions will serve similar purposes, and providing the two services in combination will reduce recidivism by less than the sum of the separately estimated parts. The important point is that the funder cannot be sure.

The simple summation of separately estimated benefits can exaggerate the total benefit for a second reason. The separately estimated pieces may well take account of the same benefit multiple times ("double counting"). For example, a funder might make a grant to a program that helps adolescents earn their GED certificates and then helps them enter job training programs. To estimate the total impact of the grant, the funder wants to capture the impact of the GED training and the impact of the follow-up job training. The temptation is to add together separate estimates from the research literature: the likely impact on future income from obtaining a GED certificate (which, according to some research, may in fact be negative), and the likely impact on income of job training.

But if the estimate of the impact of obtaining a GED certificate *already includes* the fact that obtaining a GED certificate increases the probability that the certificate holder will proceed to job training, then the addition of the two numbers will double count the impact of job training. In general, the funder won't know the extent of double counting.

The threat of miscalculation can be greatly diminished if the funder's decisions are informed by randomized controlled trials (RCTs), the best, though hardly foolproof, way to determine the impact of interventions. RCTs involve the creation of treatment and control groups by random selection from a single pool of individuals. Because the individuals in the treatment group differ from those in the control group only by the fact of treatment (or intervention), any systematic difference in outcomes between the individuals in the treatment and control groups can be attributed to the intervention under examination. But, as we explain later in the chapter, RCTs are only rarely feasible for the relatively small interventions funded by individual charities. Funders are forced to resort to less scientifically substantial procedures by which to estimate impacts.

For the common case of grants too small or otherwise unsuitable for RCTs, funders can resort to making crude correction for possible double counting. Take the preceding example about grants to programs that help high school dropouts earn their GED certificates. The funder can add estimates of the impact of the GED certificate on income to estimates of the impact of the GED certificate on the probability that a dropout will enter job training. Then, to lessen the threat of double counting, the funder can subtract, say, 10–20 percent from the total. We provide numerical examples in chapter 7.

Robin Hood confronts the problem of double counting most often for grants that affect earnings and health. For example, take interventions that promote college graduation. The studies that estimate the impact of college graduation on future earnings are separate from those that estimate college graduation on health. Adding the results of the two separate studies invites exaggeration.[4] In the absence of such studies, Robin Hood has handled the problem by making the same crude adjustment as it did in the case of the GED certificate: It subtracts 10–20 percent from the simple addition of the separate estimates. Different situations may suggest different crude adjustments. No adjustment is indisputable, but making the adjustment explicit invites both the internal and external attention that leads to better choices for the adjustment factor.

## Nonpecuniary Outcomes

The task of monetizing outcomes gets substantially harder for outcomes like health status, that don't materialize in dollars. How much value does a poverty-fighting funder create by paying lawyers to represent a poor mother fighting for custody of her children—of giving poor parents their fair day in court? And should the funder's answer depend on whether the lawyer wins the case? How much value do funders create when they find affordable apartments for families that have been forced by their financial circumstances to live "doubled up" in the cramped living space of friends or relatives? How much value is there for parents if a funder provides safe after-school programs? How much value do funders create when they help families maintain bank accounts with savings equal to, say, three months' income? What is the value of providing safe shelter to abused women and their children? And what's the toll on children of wearing tattered clothes to school or not owning a cell phone like their classmates? And how important is an emergency food program's guarantee to parents and children that they will be well fed?

There is no rock-solid answer to any of these questions. But however difficult it may be to assign explicit values to intangible outcomes, there's simply no responsible way around monetizing outcomes, including those that come in nonpecuniary form. Funders have two options. They can assign values beforehand, as called for by RM or other deliberative frameworks, or they can duck the problem and spend money by whim. But decision by whim does not avoid ranking options. The moment funders spend their money, however thoughtlessly, they've ranked the relative value of every intervention they could have afforded. The environmentalist that spends its money on saving oysters instead of saving polar bears has ranked the relative value of the two interventions. The funder may not have intended to rank options in the manner governed by whim. The funder may not be aware it has ranked options. But rank it did, the moment it made its decisions.

There are two types of errors. Error #1: The funder commits funds after explicitly monetizing nonpecuniary outcomes but does so wrongly (whatever "wrongly" might mean in this context). Error #2: The funder commits funds by some decision rule that does *not* involve explicit weightings of nonpecuniary outcomes but does so wrongly (whatever "wrongly" might mean in this context). We assert that the first kind of error is much the better of the two. Under this choice, the funder's rationale is explicitly stated, and therefore subject to debate and correction. Under Error #2, no such error correction can occur. Its mistakes are buried out of sight, now and forever.

## Resisting the Allure to Duck Options

The logic of RM is clear, but so are the challenges that confront practitioners. Monetizing dissimilar, let alone intangible, outcomes takes substantial, persistent effort. A natural response when asked to compare the proverbial apples to oranges is for the funder to duck, to allocate its grantmaking budget arbitrarily, by edict, rather than marshaling outcomes-based evidence. But ducking's like saying, "Let's not attempt to compare, in a poverty-fighting context, the value of helping high school students to graduate to the value of training ex-offenders to work as electricians. We'll choose high school students, by edict." Or, "Let's not attempt to compare, in an environmental context, the value of saving oysters in the Chesapeake Bay to the value of saving polar bears in the Arctic. We'll choose oysters, by edict." The point we emphasize here is that deciding by edict *is* to decide. To choose Option A in a world of fixed resources is to reject Option B. The (opportunity) cost of choosing Option A is the value of benefits that we could have had by funding Option B instead. The problem with edicts is that they make no attempt to weigh the value of forgone opportunities.

This problem is not limited to binary choices. A nonprofit might decide to spend preset amounts across a set of options. For example, it might decide, without scrutinizing tradeoffs, to spend 50 percent of its grant-making budget on charter schools and 50 percent on training ex-offenders. The problem has not gone away. This mode of ducking tradeoffs still fails to marshal evidence to decide whether the nonprofit's mission would be better served by discarding the 50–50 allocation in favor of, say, 60–40, 40–60, or any other split.

Of course, allocating a grant-making budget by edict greatly simplifies the funder's analytical task. And the form of the simplification is the same whether the share of the grant-making budget is set at 100 percent for one category of grant (high school students) or proportioned among two or more categories (60 percent to students and 40 percent to ex-offenders). Either way, the funder is no longer comparing the value of an education grant versus the value of an ex-offender grant. Instead, at most, the funder is left with the relatively simple task of comparing one education program to another or one ex-offender program to another. (Even this assumes that all education programs would have identical outcomes and all programs for ex-offenders also have identical outcomes, which is a strong assumption.) So rule-by-edict has reduced the funder's analytical problem to picking the education program that generates the highest number of high school graduates (relative to the number who would have graduated without the grant) per dollar of cost; and, completely separately, picking the ex-offender program that generates the biggest reduction in recidivism per dollar of cost. In neither calculation does the funder need to monetize dissimilar outcomes. The high school graduation, as outcome, is never compared with recidivism, as outcome.

Rule-by-edict is simple. That's why it is so dangerously tempting. But its simplification comes at the price of near-certain mistakes. At no point does the funder ask if it can do a lot more good by cutting its allocation to students and upping its allocation to prisoners. Ignoring tradeoffs guarantees that opportunities will be wasted.

Besides, the simplicity of ducking options enjoys a fleeting half-life. If you cannot compare education programs to job training programs because of their dissimilar outcome, can you compare two different programs for ex-offenders? How does the funder compare a program that trains unemployed female ex-offenders to become electricians to one that trains male ex-offenders to become electricians? Among education options, how does the outcome of helping students to graduate high school compare with the outcome of helping students stay enrolled once they are in college? Posed another way, if funders are to duck comparing dissimilar programs, won't they be left with comparing nearly nothing? Few outcomes are truly identical. The funder that eschews comparing programs with dissimilar outcomes—eschews RM—will be left with very little to do indeed.

Nothing (exceptional circumstances aside) forces an environmental funder to rule out saving oysters. Nothing forces a poverty-fighting funder to split its budget 50–50 between education and job training programs. If funders make such arbitrary "top-down" decisions, they rule out by assumption potential powerhouse interventions. That's a monster price to pay for a simpler job.

To make the point vividly, consider an opposite case—a case in which the funder has no right to compare options. The Daniels Fund makes program grants across four states (Colorado, New Mexico, Utah, and Wyoming) and nine program categories (including aging, amateur sports, early childhood education, and youth development). The key point is that grant funding, in the words of the fund's Web site, "is allocated across our four states, as well as to some national programs, according to percentages established by Bill Daniels," the benefactor of the fund. In this case, the funder need not develop ways to compare the relative impact of programs run in New Mexico versus Utah because the benefactor has ruled out any such transfers. Where tradeoffs are disallowed, monetization of outcomes plays no role.

That said, the fund does need to decide exactly which programs to fund within each state. Take the challenge of deciding which sports programs to fund. Do all programs that come under the mantle "amateur sports" share an identical outcome? Not likely. The foundation is saddled with the task of comparing the value of nonidentical outcomes of programs within program categories. So the staff of the Daniels Fund finds itself in the thick soup of monetizing nonidentical outcomes. No escape.

The important point is that the strategy of ducking comparisons breaks apart rather quickly. In fact, ducking the job of comparing options does not make them disappear. Funders that ignore options risk betraying the mission for which they are responsible.

# 4

# Those Pesky Counterfactuals

Until now, we've elided the biggest obstacle to smart monetization: taking proper account of "counterfactual" information, an essential ingredient for measuring the impact of a philanthropic intervention. We now correct that omission.

Estimating counterfactual figures is a messy, complicated business, the most challenging part of metrics by far. But if funders are to do their job of estimating impacts on a cause-and-effect basis, there's no getting around the problem. Anything else is burying one's proverbial head deep into the sand. The funder's technique need not be scientifically elegant. Nor, as we'll show, need the estimates cost a crippling amount in staff time or money. But in any case, the funder needs to tackle the task forthrightly and transparently because estimates of counterfactuals disproportionately affect the funder's assessment of its interventions.

Here's a thought experiment. A funder contemplates a grant to XYZ high school for the sole purpose of raising the percentage of low-income New Yorkers who earn their high school diploma. (Note that this narrow aim includes no academic impacts other than graduation.) The funder's interest in XYZ starts with the fact that it graduates 99 percent of its students, very nearly all of whom do so ready to enter college courses. By contrast, the citywide graduation rate is around 65 percent, and only a small fraction of those graduates qualify for college. So far, XYZ sounds like a great school to back, with graduation rates more than 30 percentage points above the citywide average, and a great candidate for grant support.

Let's add some information. Suppose XYZ's real name is Stuyvesant High School, the nationally renowned high school in New York City that admits only the city's academically best students. The funder could reasonably surmise that Stuyvesant's students were headed for academic success no matter which high school they attended. Otherwise, they would never have gained admission to Stuyvesant. By this surmise, Stuyvesant's students would have graduated high school even without Stuyvesant's help (though Stuyvesant might well improve the academic achievement of its students in ways other than graduation). The impact of Stuyvesant on graduation rates is closer to zero than to 30 percentage points, a huge difference.

This is a crystal clear example of the crucial role in program analysis played by counterfactual information. A funder whose mission is to prevent poverty best estimates the poverty-reducing impact of a high school by estimating the *difference* between: (1) XYZ's *actual* graduation rate and (2) XYZ's *counterfactual graduation rate*: the graduation rate of XYZ's students had they enrolled in neighboring schools instead.

Here's the problem. Counterfactual figures, as called for in (2), by definition cannot be observed. No one can observe what the graduation rate of XYZ's students would have been had they attended some other high school for the simple reasons that XYZ's students attend XYZ (yes, President Grant truly is buried in Grant's tomb). Thus, the challenge: how to estimate that which cannot be observed. Estimation requires theories—theories of what could best be expected to happen to program participants had they not so participated. In the case of XYZ, we would invoke the rich literature on graduation rates of students whose demographic characteristics mirror those of Stuyvesant's students.

Let's digress to make a powerful point. *Any* statement about the impact of interventions, historical or otherwise, requires making assumptions about counterfactual information. The only option that evaluators have is whether to make their counterfactual assumptions explicit. Pundits often draw conclusions about the impact of programs without stating their assumptions. Shame on them. They're hiding key information from public scrutiny or, perhaps, even from themselves.

Take a simple claim, one that at first glance appears to involve no counterfactual information. A historian claims that Thomas Jefferson was a great president of the United States because he completed the purchase of the Louisiana Territory. That's a definitive judgment. It appears to skirt counterfactual data. But take a second glance. The historian who judges the Louisiana Purchase as an act of presidential brilliance is making the implicit assumption that John Adams, President Jefferson's opponent in the 1800 election, or other plausible presidents, might well have failed to capitalize on the opportunity. After all, no historian would cite bumper wheat crops in the mid-1960s as a reason to judge Lyndon Johnson a great president because no historian would attribute the bumper crops to any special presidential action. Is the judgment about President Jefferson correct? We'll pose as agnostic because the point here is analytical, not historical. To proclaim President Jefferson's brilliance implies a judgment about unobservable information: what John Adams would have done in Jefferson's circumstances.

Let's take a slightly more modern example. During the latter part of the 2012 presidential election, critics of President Obama's stimulus legislation said it did not work because the immediate pre-election unemployment rate (around 8 percent) was no lower than it was at the time the bill was passed. But that's irrelevant. The comparison that needed to be made was not the actual October 2012 unemployment rate versus the actual rate when the stimulus bill was passed. The right comparison was between the October 2012 unemployment rate and the unemployment rate that *would* have prevailed today had the stimulus bill *not* been passed (counterfactual rate). If without the bill, the October 2012 unemployment rate would have been 15 percent rather than its actual level of 8 percent, then we'd all agree the bill had been a major success. Comparing the immediate pre-election actual unemployment rate to the actual rate two years ago proves exactly nothing. Our point is not that the stimulus bill was or was not successful. Our point is that the public policy debate about the bill's impact misses the point entirely. Every example we provided earlier in this chapter, and for the remainder of this book, must be placed in the context of judging success or impact the right way, with explicit and careful attention to counterfactual numbers.

In the first instance, before XYZ high school was identified, the funder assumed that the students at XYZ were roughly similar to the students in neighboring high schools, and, therefore, that they would have graduated at rates comparable to students at local schools (around 65 percent). By that counterfactual, XYZ's program looks spectacularly successful (99 percent at XYZ vs. 65 percent otherwise).

In the second instance, once we learn that XYZ is in fact Stuyvesant, then the counterfactual estimate changes dramatically. The kind of students who gain admission to Stuyvesant would no doubt graduate at a rate of 99 percent or so no matter what high school they attended. So under this revised counterfactual graduation rate, the "Stuyvesant effect" on graduation would look inconsequential.

The following example cries out to funders to make their counterfactual assumptions explicit, and therefore challengeable.

Take two job training groups that train women to set up day care operations in their homes. Let's assume that all women who set up operations earn about $10,000 a year. Nonprofit Apple graduates 80 percent of its enrollees, of whom 70 percent go on to set up operations. Therefore, about 55 percent of its enrollees set up day care operations in their homes. Nonprofit Banana graduates only 60 percent of its enrollees, of whom only 50 percent set up operations. Therefore, about 30 percent of its enrollees set up their own day care operations.

Which is better, Apple or Banana? The glib answer is Apple, whose success rate is 25 percentage points higher than that of Banana. But the right answer is that you can't tell.

Let's add some information. Apple's enrollees earned an average of $8,000 a year before entering the training program. Banana's enrollees, mostly abused women, earned nearly nothing during the year before they entered training. Thus, Apple boosted the income of 55 percent of its graduates by about $2,000 per year (to $10,000 from $8,000). Of every 100 enrollees, that amounts to boosting the collective income of the enrollees by $110,000 (55 successes × $2,000/success). Banana, by contrast, boosted the income of 30 percent of its graduates by a whopping $10,000 per year. Of every 100 enrollees, that amounts to boosting the collective income of the enrollees by $300,000. Banana wins by a landslide.[1]

The thought experiment makes the vivid point that counterfactual numbers—in this case, the different estimates of expected earnings boost based on different demographic characteristics of the enrollees—make a huge difference for evaluation. Graduation and placement rates matter, but in this case, those numbers are wholly misleading. The lower success rate of Banana is more than offset by the bigger impact it has on each of its highly disadvantaged enrollees.

Too few funders lay out explicit counterfactual figures—how much of any change in the circumstances of their participants would have happened in the absence of the funder's intervention. In the preceding case, let's assume that the pretraining income of participants provides a good guide as to their earnings if the participants had not enrolled in the training program. In the case of the participants in Apple, $8,000 of the $10,000 final income of the day care workers would have happened even without the new training. In this case, inattention to counterfactuals is self-serving. Inattention amounts to assuming that every dollar earned by a participant is actually the result of the funder's intervention, which is a massive, self-serving exaggeration. Indeed, if the funder had been forthright and stated explicitly that it would assume that none of the $10,000 earned by graduates would have been earned without the day care training, the reader would see through the charade.

Our last example points to the need for funders to comb the literature for the correct counterfactual estimates.

Take a job training program that teaches unemployed workers to remove environmentally toxic materials from construction sites. The graduates earn, on average, $15 an hour. As in the previous examples, to measure success the funder needs to compare (1) *actual* earnings of trainees after graduation and (2) *counterfactual earnings*: earnings of trainees if they, in fact, had not entered the job training program. For (2), the evaluator of the program needs to adopt a set of assumptions—in other words, what social scientists call a model—that specify what the evaluator assumes the trainees would have earned without training. Some such models are simple. Others are complicated. In every case, evaluators need to come clean about the assumptions they make about the prospects of trainees had they not been trained.

A simple model of counterfactual earnings might assume that trainees would earn in the future, without training, what they had earned the year or so before they were trained (often referred to as "baseline data"). Baseline data do exist and can often be observed. But using baseline data to proxy for counterfactual data is also making an assumption. It's a model that says past is prologue. The problem is that the model is often wrong, and even self-serving. The assumption that an individual's future earnings would mirror current earnings often serves to exaggerate the impact of interventions. Recent research on job training programs isn't kind to simple models of that ilk.

To see why, let's take a look at the evidence from RCTs on the effectiveness of job training programs. As discussed, RCTs eliminate the problem of adopting a model of behavior by which to create counterfactual estimates. In RCTs, the treatment and control groups are deliberately selected so as to have very similar characteristics, which allows the outcomes of the control group to serve as a good proxy for the counterfactual outcomes of the treatment group; that is, the outcomes of members of the treatment group had they, counter to fact, not received treatment. Then, after conducting the RCT, the evaluator can derive an estimate of the impact of the program, relative to a statistically defensible counterfactual, simply by comparing the observed outcomes of members of the treatment group (those who receive job training) to observed outcomes of the statistically identical members of the control group (who receive no job training).

What we've learned from the RCTs that have been performed is both important and sobering, and it spotlights the danger of using baseline data to define the counterfactual. Typically, in RCTs of job training programs, the incomes of members of the treatment group rise over time. That is what we hope for and expect. But the incomes of the *control group* also can rise over time. That seems counterintuitive and certainly unexpected.[2]

If the training is useful, then the incomes of members of the treatment group rise at a rate faster than for the control group. But the fact that future earnings of members of the control group systematically exceed their baseline earnings (earnings before the date when the treatment group receives training) means that the evaluators who use baseline earnings to serve as proxy for counterfactual earnings will underestimate counterfactual earnings. The implication is that the use of baseline earnings as a proxy for counterfactual earnings systematically overestimates the gap between actual future earnings and counterfactual earnings of trainees, thereby exaggerating the impact of the training program. In other words, the tendency is for evaluators (and the funders for whom they work) to think their programs are better than they truly are.

As an example, let's assume: (1) Chronically unemployed workers who apply for job training are currently earning nothing ($0). (2) These applicants would, in the absence of finding a job training slot, scramble for unskilled work, earning $2,000/year. (3) After training, the applicants earn $5,000/year. Under the default assumption that baseline earnings are the funder's best estimate of counterfactual earnings, the funder would estimate that job training boosts annual earnings by $5,000 (= $5,000 − $0). But counterfactual earnings here are $2,000, not $0. Job training in fact increases annual earnings by only $3,000 (= $5,000 − $2,000). The all-too-common default assumption exaggerates the impact of the intervention, giving the funder a bloated sense of its impact.

Why do earnings of people who receive no training (the control group) systematically rise over time? The answer is selection bias. The control group is composed of individuals who volunteer for job training but do not get selected. Who volunteers for training? In general, the folks who line up for training often have made a decision to turn their lives around, one way or another. If they don't gain entrance to the particular job traininge program under review, they will volunteer for another such program. Or they will take some other action that will produce higher earnings tomorrow than they earned last year.

*Does this mean that smart philanthropy requires an RCT for every initiative? No way.* For almost all funders and donors, RCTs are a luxury.

RCTs are expensive and time consuming. And by the time they are complete, the program under review, or the social context within which the program operates, may well have changed dramatically. Hence, they are performed infrequently, especially when small grants or small programs are involved—like the grants made by the most funders. But if RCTs are often impractical, and simple models of counterfactual earnings, such as baseline earnings, don't suffice, are we at an evaluative impasse? No. The research literature is littered with estimates that funders can use, with a pinch of creativity, to form plausible counterfactual estimates. And if published research fails to provide the exact numbers that funders need, it often provides sufficiently close substitutes. Lots of high-quality research papers shed evidentiary light on how much individuals earn based on their demographic and other characteristics. So too, whole journals are devoted to estimating how much students of various demographic stripes will earn. And so on.

The important point is that evidence-based estimates of counterfactuals, however imperfect, exist for the taking. They beat the self-serving practice of citing no explicit counterfactual estimates (as the preceding examples amply demonstrate). We provide concrete examples in chapters 6 and 7 of how Robin Hood estimates counterfactual figures for the interventions that it funds.

The general strategy is clear. Funders pay grantees to deliver services to needy individuals (human or otherwise). Those services might be designed, for example, to save an endangered species, teach graphic arts to elementary public school children, end bullying on school playgrounds, or teach occupational skills to unemployed workers. Take the latter example. To gauge success, first measure the actual outcome (say, earnings) of each treated individual. Second, estimate each individual's counterfactual outcome, using an explicit model by which to estimate unobservable data. Third, estimate success for each treated individual by estimating the difference between each individual's actual outcome and that individual's counterfactual outcome. Fourth, estimate success for the grant in its entirety by adding together the estimates of success for each individual.

In common instances, data on *individuals* receiving services will not be available. But average outcomes for the *group* of individuals who receive services will be known, as might the average counterfactual outcomes for the group. In such circumstances, an estimate of the impact of the grant can be estimated, first, by subtracting the average counterfactual outcome from the average observed outcome of treated individuals. That subtraction provides an estimate of average impact (or success). Multiplying the average impact by the number of treated individuals provides an estimate of the grant's total impact/success.

(For grants of individual funders, as opposed to massive programs funded by government, the success of the grant will most often [although not always] be well estimated as the simple sum of individual successes. Externalities [third-party effects] of the kind that could make the whole impact differ substantially from the sum of the individual parts are rare.)

In the case of Robin Hood, staff in effect makes two estimates for each grant. First, what would the collective living standards (earnings plus a monetized value of health status) of poor New Yorkers be if the proposed grant were made? Second, what would the collective living standards of poor New Yorkers be if the grant were not made? The difference between these two estimates captures the impact of the grant and forms the numerator of the grant's benefit/cost estimate. This way of describing the process emphasizes the cause-and-effect mentality. Robin Hood is not the sole cause of successes racked up by grantees. The question in every case is how much success does Robin Hood's grant create, all else being the same (those nasty words again—meaning, assuming no surprising changes such as substantial changes in funding by other private and public funders). Said another way, how much would the collective living standards of poor New Yorkers fall if Robin Hood were to withdraw its grant (all else being the same).

The calculations are often far from straightforward. One devilish problem is that of displacement or other types of systemwide feedback effects.

Here's another thought experiment. MicroL makes microloans to poor entrepreneurs. What's the impact of a $1,500 loan to Harry to expand his dry cleaning store on 12th and First Avenue? Assessment involves the usual set of hard-to-solve problems. How much more will Harry make after expansion? How would Harry's earnings have changed even without the microloan from MicroL? And so on. But there's a systemwide complication. Where do Harry's extra clients come from?

If his new customers come at the expense of a dry cleaning operator at 12th and Second Avenue, driving that operator out of business and into poverty, then MicroL's loans are not so much fighting poverty as they are picking winners. MicroL's borrower won't be as poor, but some non-poor entrepreneur on 12th street will be newly poor. In a similar vein, does a microloan to Lucy to set up a hairdressing operation in her basement take business away from an equally poor entrepreneur, Harriet, down the street? If so, the microloan does nothing to cut poverty. The loan picks which hairdresser will be poor and which will be non-poor, but the microloan will not have reduced poverty.

There are not the only counterfactual issues at the systemwide level. Suppose a funder is contemplating a grant to HireL, a well-established program that trains unemployed welfare recipients to do carpentry. In one version of this grant, the funder covers the cost of training two carpenters ($5,000 each, for a total cost of $10,000), each of whom earns $15,000 more over their lifetime because of the training. That comes to a benefit/cost ratio of about 3:1. In version two, the training program can draw on $2 of state and federal grants for every $1 put up by the funder. That creates a benefit/cost ratio about three times higher, around 9:1.

But not so fast. The funder needs to ask, what's the counterfactual? If HireL draws down the state and federal funds, does that lead to some other job training program drawing down fewer dollars, leading it to train fewer welfare recipients? Again, has the funder reduced poverty, or merely changed the name of the person who wallows in poverty?

Another complicating wrinkle is that funders join forces in funding grantees. Such partnerships complicate the estimation of counterfactual numbers. For readers who want to dig deeper, we examine some of these issues in appendix A.

What's the reader to make of these complications? Counterfactual estimating is hard but necessary. It's not enough to mouth the words Relentless Monetization. It's important to carefully implement the framework. The proverbial slip between the cup of RM and the lip of correctly implemented RM is vast.

# 5

# The Meaning of Present Discounted Values

Because the notion of present discounted values emerges at several junctures in this book, this chapter examines the idea in more detail.

Some initiatives yield all their benefits at about the same time that the funder initially spends money. Emergency food is an example, assuming that the nutrition from the meal does not yield a lasting health benefit. Most initiatives, however, generate benefits over extended periods of time, even decades. Job training and early childhood programs come to mind. To choose among long-acting initiatives, funders need a framework that takes systematic account of differences in the timing of benefits and costs.

The analytical tool for doing so is called present discounted value (PDV) or, the equivalent, discounted present value (DPV). PDV starts from a simple premise. Funders, like everyone else, prefer benefits that accrue immediately to identical benefits that accrue in the future. We cite three rationales for the premise.

First, impatience. Why put off to tomorrow a pleasure that can be enjoyed today? Second, aversion to risk. If a benefit accrues today, you have it for sure. But if you postpone that benefit until the future, something might occur between now and then to prevent you from ever enjoying the benefit you could have enjoyed earlier. Third, compound interest. If the benefit comes in the form of money, you can take control of the dollars today, invest them, and have even more dollars in the future.

Let's play out this third rationale. No one would pay $100 for the privilege of receiving $100 one year hence (even if the payment were guaranteed). If, for example, you could earn a safe 10 percent return on your money, the most that you would pay today in return for a payment of $100 a year from today would be $90.91 because $90.91 is the amount you would need to invest today at a 10 percent rate of return to have $100 one year hence [$90.91 + (0.10) × ($90.91) = $100]. A little additional algebra tells us that it would take an investment of only $82.64 today to generate $100 two years hence. ($82.64 grows to nearly $90.91 after one year and to $100 after two years.) In the jargon of economists, if the interest rate is 10%, $90.91 is the present discounted value (PDV) of $100 to be received one year hence and $82.64 is the PDV of $100 to be received two years hence. By extension, the PDV of receiving two payments, $100 one year from today and another $100 two years from today, is the sum of the PDVs of the two payments, in this case, $173.55 ( = $90.91 + $82.64). In other words, once you specify an interest rate with which to "discount" benefits that accrue in the future, PDV gives you the value today of a flow of benefits (here, "payments") that will accrue over time.

Similar algebraic logic can convert any stream of future benefits, however erratic, into a single number. That single number equals the amount of money that would need to be invested immediately to generate the particular stream of future benefits under review. In the first example, $90.91 is that single number. The rate at which investments are assumed to grow—10 percent in the preceding example—is called the "discount rate." In practice, that rate might reflect the rates that the funder can earn on invested money. Or it might reflect the impatience of funders: if they cannot generate 20 percent rates of return on projects, they just as soon invest nothing at all. By the logic of compound interest, discounting (as the process is called for calculating the current value of a future stream of benefits) makes little difference if the future is not far from the present. But benefits far into the future will be worth surprisingly little when the discount rate is above a nontrivial level. For example, with a discount rate of 10 percent, the present discounted value of a $100,000 benefit to be delivered 25 years hence would be only about $9,500. If the $100,000 benefit were to accrue 50 years out, then the PDV would fall to a measly $900.

Consider calculating the present discounted value of a high school diploma, assuming the graduate does not proceed on to college. Research tells us that high school graduates will earn an average of $6,500 a year more than dropouts with similar demographic characteristics. Over the course of a 50-year career (age 18–68), if we use a discount rate of 3 percent per year, the PDV of those annual $6,500 additions to income (the benefit) amounts to about $173,743. In other words, it would take $173,743 invested today in relatively safe financial instrument to generate $6,500 a year over the next 50 years.

Let's take note that calculating present discounted values requires making a number of assumptions, and these assumptions can sway the calculations by large amounts. For starters, if we performed no discounting at all and simply added together 50 earnings increments of $6,500 each, then we'd arrive at a figure of $325,000. If, instead, we used a discount rate of 5 percent rather than 3 percent, the present discounted value falls to $125,000. Higher discount rates translate to lower PDVs. And if we shorten the length of time that we expect the earnings boost to last (relative to earnings of high school dropouts), then the $125,000 figure would drop further. Robin Hood uses a present discounted value of $100,000 to capture the impact of a high school diploma.

Discounting of future benefits has another important implication. As funders quantify the impact of their interventions, whether by relentless monetization (RM) or some other framework, they can ignore with impunity uncertain benefits that might accrue generations into the future. The present discounted value of such benefits approaches zero. Too see this, consider the aggregate value of a stream of annual payments of $100 that lasts forever. (Forever is a silly assumption, but it makes the arithmetic Simple Simon.) One might be tempted to assign an astronomical value. After all, over the first 300 years alone, total payments would amount to $30,000 ($100/year × 300 years). But any such calculation ignores that all-important fact that dollars to be delivered in the future are not worth as much as a dollar delivered today. Indeed, if the bank interest rate is 5 percent, we would need to have just $2,000 deposited today—a far cry from $30,000, much less an astronomical sum—to generate, at a 5 percent rate of interest, a flow of $100 a year forever ($2000 × 0.05/year = $100/year). Therefore, the stream of $100 annual payments for all eternity is worth only about $2,000 because that is all that needs to be invested today to generate the future stream of $100 yearly payments. (Perhaps that explains why a college won't name itself after a donor that offers it a gift of $1 billion payable at the rate of $1,000 a year for the next million years.)

In the real world, the computation of present discounted values requires that we make some choices: the interest rate, the assumed inflation
rate, and the pattern of the stream of benefits over time, including the
length of time that the benefits will last. As illustration, to calculate the
PDV of a high school education, the funder would need to estimate how
long the high school graduate will continue to earn $6,500/year more than
a demographically similar dropout (a question that research can partially
answer). As we saw, an earnings boost that lasts 50 years would imply a
PDV of almost $175,000 if we apply a discount rate of 3% per year. But if
the career were only 20 years, the PDV would fall to about $100,000. We've
assumed here that the increment to income, $6,500, is the same every year.
In some cases, we might imagine that the increment could vary over time.
No problem. No matter how complicated the computation, the interpreta-
tion is always the same. The present discounted value of a particular stream
of dollar benefits always equals the number of dollars that would need to be
invested today, at some particular interest rate, to generate that particular
stream.

Properly discounting future benefits as part of RM is all in the interest
of making better choices in allocating resources. It follows that a funder's
choice of discount rate must be made with care—just how much less *do* we
value benefits that accrue further into the future—and that a funder should
use a consistent discount rate when it assesses the benefits of the various
interventions it could fund. And given the powerful impact of the choice
of discount rate on the PDV of interventions that yield their benefits over
time, transparency requires that the choice of discount rate be explicit and
available for all to see.

Chapter 6 moves from the theory behind the RM framework to numerical examples.

# 6

# Examples of Metrics by Outcome

In this chapter, we set out the equations by which we assign mission-relevant value to individual outcomes generated by a funder's grant. What is the monetary value of helping ex-offenders graduate high school? What is the monetary value of training ex-offenders to work as drug-abuse counselors? We leave to chapter 7 the discussion of monetizing entire grants, which we take to be a combination of outcomes: Example: what is the monetary value of a grant that both helps ex-offenders earn their high school diplomas and then trains them to work as substance abuse counselors?[1]

Before we get started, we remind readers that grant decisions, as discussed in chapter 1, need to weigh benefits *and* costs. The next two chapters focus solely on benefits (the numerators of benefit/cost ratios). *Because the discussion that follows ignores costs, it cannot by itself be used to make smart grant decisions.* That exercise awaits chapter 8.

As will become clear, the same program applied to different target groups constitutes, for purposes of doing metrics, two different interventions. Take the case of a high school curriculum that's adopted by two schools with the aim of boosting graduation rates of at-risk students. One school serves ex-offenders, and the other school serves dropouts with no criminal involvement. These two different populations experience different counterfactual graduation rates. And different counterfactual graduation rates generate different estimates of the value of the grant.

In Robin Hood's case, staff has set down equations that monetize the impact of each of more than 170 distinct mission-relevant outcomes. Associated with each equation is a rationale for each coefficient in the equation with reference to the source of the estimates. Many coefficients come from research literature. Others come from data collected by grantees. And some reflect educated guesswork only.

Here are some examples of the 170 or so distinct mission-relevant outcomes that arise from grants that Robin Hood funds.

Acquiring a high school diploma

Acquiring a GED certificate, with no further education

Acquiring a GED certificate followed by at least one year of college follow-up

Acquiring legal order of protection for an abused spouse

Overturning eviction notices

Overturning school's refusal to pay for programs to address a child's learning disability

Enrolling unemployed workers for unemployment insurance

Enrolling disabled workers for federal disability payments

Enrolling low-paid workers for federal, state, and city tax refunds

Extending microloans to Iraq/Afghanistan vets, leading to setting up of home businesses

Preventing first arrest of criminally at-risk youth

Improving a client's credit score through financial counseling

Preparing a client to file for bankruptcy with the help of financial counseling

Providing showers, haircuts, and mailboxes to visitors of emergency-food programs

Reducing deaths caused by substance abuse

Detecting colon cancer in men early through screening

Teaching carpentry skills to formerly incarcerated workers

Teaching carpentry skills to immigrants with high school diplomas

Training first-time parents

Helping victims of domestic violence recover from major physical injuries

Helping victims of domestic violence deal with posttraumatic stress disorder (PTSD)

Tutoring to raise students' standardized test scores

Treating school-age children's asthma

Helping Iraq/Afghanistan vets find and keep employment by treating
their PTSD

And so on.

The entries reflect the practice of defining interventions as narrowly as possible. The metrics that govern financial counseling for the purpose of improving a family's credit score are different from the metrics for financial counseling for the purpose of declaring bankruptcy, even if the content of the financial counseling is roughly the same in both cases. The poverty-fighting value of teaching formerly incarcerated workers to become entry-level carpenters is different from the value of teaching the exact same skill to Ecuadorian immigrants with high school diplomas from their home countries.

The common thread is that similar interventions for dissimilar populations amount to distinct interventions, requiring different calculations to track impact. In other words, estimating counterfactual values is an essential part of the process of monetizing outcomes.

Some of the previously listed outcomes, like keeping schoolchildren out of emergency rooms by treating their asthma, cry out for measurement because the impacts on school performance and future employment are likely profound. But what does providing showers and haircuts to visitors to food pantries and soup kitchens accomplish? Is there some indisputable "correct" figure? No. But consider this. If the funder fails to monetize showers and makes resource allocation decisions on the basis of monetized outcomes, it is equivalent to treating showers as having no value at all. Then program officers will cut the money for them out of future grants. Is that the right decision? Our point here is that the correct first step is to monetize, *then* decide about funding. Showers and haircuts are light-touch interventions by any metric. They don't transform anyone's life. But showers and haircuts are cheap. The question—which we address at length in chapter 8—is whether the services generate enough value to more than justify their cost. Do showers and haircuts generate more value than the same amount of money would generate if used somewhere else? Smart philanthropists don't assume answers. They base them on the best information it is practical to obtain.

Funders often skip the slippery task of monetizing nonpecuniary outcomes. In practice, that means they either assign no value to the nonpecuniary outcomes, which is hardly an inspiring way to proceed; or they assume, without recourse to evidence, that the nonpecuniary outcomes are hugely valuable and worthy of funding, which is also hardly an inspiring way to proceed. School-based anti-bullying programs are all the recent rage, perhaps for good reason. They sound great. But what's the evidence that such programs have long-term consequences?

Robin Hood plans to put its equations on its Web site during 2013. We present two of them in the following section. We focus on the gist of the equations rather than the details.

## Intervention 1. The Value of Graduating High School

Robin Hood makes a grant to a charter middle school for the primary purpose of increasing the percentage of students who earn high school diplomas. It does so because students who earn their high school diplomas take a powerful step out of poverty.

The key ingredients to calculating the impact on the future earnings of students of the middle school grant:

(##): *Observed* number of the middle school's eighth-grade students. In general, the school provides the number to Robin Hood; no estimation needed.

(AA): *Observed* percentage of the middle school's eighth graders who go on to graduate from high school within 4–6 years, as reported by the school or school system. But here the funder runs into trouble. A middle school won't usually know which of its former students graduate from high school. If the middle school students stay in the same public school system, then the school system may well provide the information. Or the middle school, perhaps with the financial help of Robin Hood, may track its graduates. But if many middle school students leave the school district, the problem of collecting accurate data on future high school graduation arises. For the charter middle schools that Robin Hood supports in New York City, about 85 percent or so of the students go on to graduate from high school.

(BB): *Estimated* rate of graduation if Robin Hood had not made its grant: the counterfactual graduation rate. The figure may be taken from data on actual high school graduation rates for students attending traditional middle schools in the charter middle school's neighborhood, especially for students of similar demographic characteristics. This number cannot be observed; it must be estimated on the basis of a set of assumptions. The obvious starting point is to note that in New York City, about 65 percent of public school students graduate high school. But counterfactual estimates are virtually never straightforward. For example, the city's school authorities define graduation rates differently from state authorities. And individual schools can use a wholly different definition. Is 65 percent the right counterfactual figure? Almost certainly not. The graduation rate for students of the same demographic characteristics as those of Robin Hood's grant recipients is lower across the city's poor neighborhoods—closer to 50 percent than 65 percent. Members of Robin Hood's staff have spent months tussling over the right figures to use. Yes, their self-interest is a hazard: The lower the counterfactual rate, the more effective a program officer's middle school grant will appear to be. But having explicit assumptions that are open to all for inspection is the best antidote to self-serving exaggeration.

(CC): *Estimated* earnings boost for students who do not proceed to college: The difference between the earnings of students who graduate from high school and the earnings of demographically similar students who fail to graduate. Here, too, there is no one place to look up this number. The counterfactual number must be estimated. Sometimes, Robin Hood's relies upon its full-time researcher or program officers to recommend an estimate based on their scan of the evidence. Or Robin Hood hires external consultants to do original research or pore over peer-reviewed studies before recommending figures for estimated impacts.

On education, Robin Hood chose the latter route. Based on professional consultants, Robin Hood uses $6,500 per year as its estimate of the earnings boost resulting from high school graduation. This estimate applies to students who do not later enroll in college.

(DD): *Estimated* number of years over which the annual earnings boost lasts. Robin Hood for now assumes 20 years. But this assumption is under review as Robin Hood seeks additional relevant research findings.

(EE): Value of lifetime health improvement per high school graduate. Students who graduate high school live longer, healthier lives than do demographically similar students who drop out. Outside consultants found that graduation leads to an increase in health status of 1.8 quality adjusted life years (QALYs). Robin Hood, as we explained in chapter 3, monetizes health status at $50,000 per QALY. Therefore, the medical benefit of a student graduating high school rather than dropping out is worth an estimated $90,000 (= 1.8 QALY × $50,000/QALY).

(FF): *Observed/estimated* percentage of students who enroll in college. Data provided by follow-up surveys conducted by the middle school grant recipient.

(GG): *Estimated* percentage of those students who would have graduated high school who would then have also completed a year of college even in the absence of Robin Hood's grant to its charter middle school (counterfactual rate). Robin Hood assumes that percentage to be 50 percent. The estimate is based on the college attendance figures in traditional public schools across New York City.

(HH) Earnings boost from a year of college. Peer-reviewed research, as examined by consultants hired by Robin Hood, indicates that for students with demographic characteristics similar to those in schools funded by Robin Hood, attending college for at least one year adds about $2,500 a year to earnings.

(JJ): *Estimated* number of years over which the annual earnings boost for college attendees lasts. Robin Hood for now assumes 20 years (the same as for those who do not attend college, despite the fact that attendees enter the labor force a year or two later). Here too the assumption is under review as Robin Hood seeks additional relevant research findings.

Here's the governing equation:

Poverty-Fighting Benefit from Raising High School Graduation Rate = Present discounted value of:

$$\text{Equation 1: } [\#] \times [\text{AA\%} - \text{BB\%}] \times [\$\text{CC} \times \text{DD} + \text{EE}]$$
$$+ [\#] \times [\text{FF\%} - \text{GG\%}] \times \text{HH} \times \text{JJ}]$$

Some typical numbers from Robin Hood's experience:

\# = 100 students; AA = 85%; BB = 50%; CC = $6,500/year; DD = 20 years; EE = $90,000; FF = 60%; GG = 50%; HH = $2500; JJ = 20 years.

For a charter middle school, the total might be $7 million (plus or minus). We warn the reader against comparing the total for any one school against that of any other because this calculation takes no account of costs. We tackle the issue of costs in chapter 8. Without factoring in costs, we cannot conclude whether $7 million (or whatever the total benefit turns out to be) is high or low.

To the extent that the rough numbers used in this example reflect reality, the arithmetic says grants to middle schools generate sizeable health benefits for low-income families. As we'll see in chapter 7, this fact pushes education-related grants ahead of many other ways of fighting poverty. That's exactly what the funder wants its metrics system to do—drive grants dollars to the highest valued use. Said another way, the results cry out to funders to monetize health when making decisions about education-related grants. Otherwise, intentionally or not, the funder would be counting health benefits as if they were of zero value and thereby systematically undervalue the impact of education-related grants. Reasonable folks can debate what number to assign to the value of a QALY. But just because the right value for measuring the value of changes in health status is hard to pin down ought to give no funder license to treat the value of those changes as zero. For a poverty-fighting funder to ignore the impact on health is fundamentally mistaken. RM allows for no such oversight.

Let's note how the equation would change if the grantee were to serve a different demographic group. We cite two differences.

First, counterfactual earnings. Compare the preceding equation for a charter middle school to the equation that would apply to an intervention that would financially support students at a "transfer school." Transfer schools serve disadvantaged students who have been previously expelled from traditional high schools. Graduating a student from a transfer school might do more poverty-fighting good than would graduating a student from a traditional or charter public school if, as is likely, counterfactual earnings—the expected future earnings of students who attend transfer schools—fall far below counterfactual earnings of students who attend nontransfer schools. Translation: BB, the counterfactual graduation rate, would be substantially lower for these high school dropouts, probably closer to 15 percent than 50 percent.

Second, graduation rates. The transfer school's graduation rate would almost certainly fall short of the graduation rate of a typical traditional middle school (a school that does not reach out to dropouts). These two differences in the equations for transfer schools versus charter middle schools move the estimated benefit in opposite directions. The point to note here is that RM metrics—the arithmetic behind Equation 1—takes proper account of all the key noncost variables. RM will tilt toward the transfer school if its graduation rate doesn't fall *too far* below that of the charter school. Equation 1 accounts for these tradeoffs in seamless manner.

Indeed, RM can drive funders into seemingly strange places. Take the case of two $100,000 grants to a 100-student charter middle school and a 100-student transfer school, respectively. Assume that the charter middle school boosts the number of high school graduates by 35 percentage points, to 85 percent from 50 percent. Assume that the transfer school boosts the number of high school graduates by 20 percentage points, to 35 percent from 15 percent. Whether looking at the absolute number of graduates or even the change in the number of high school graduates, the transfer school looks like a loser. But if—as is quite possible, given the dreadful prospects of students who have been kicked out of high school—the income boost from graduating from the transfer school dwarfs the income boost from graduating from a charter middle school, then RM will drive the funder to support the "loser." Exactly right.

Next, consider how the equation would change if the grantee were an early childhood program rather than a middle school or transfer school. Studies of the long-term impacts of model early child hood programs indicate that high quality pre-kindergarten programs can boost the future high school graduation rates of children. But the impacts are uncertain and not well understood. After all, 15 years or so intervene between the pre-kindergarten interventions and poverty-related outcomes (do the students graduate high school on time?). That has made early childhood programs very expensive to study. Indeed, as previously mentioned, the uncertainty surrounding the impact of early childhood programs has led Robin Hood, in partnership with MDRC, to set up an institute to run randomized controlled trials to test the long-term impact of pre-kindergarten interventions. That said, peer-reviewed studies of model early childhood programs indicate that they boost high school graduation rates by about 30 percent. Model programs also decrease future criminality and increase future earnings. Robin Hood users these findings to develop metrics equations similar to Equation 1.

Finally, RM requires flexibility and ingenuity. Consider how the analysis would need to change if a grant were made to a new middle school with an experimental program. Assume there is no evidence on which to base an estimate of the future high school graduation rates. The funder might estimate the future graduation rates of the students by borrowing graduation rates of middle schools that most closely resemble the grant recipient. But if the school is new and the program is experimental, there might well be no other schools that resemble the grantee. In that case, the funder will need to base metrics on a variable other than graduation rates.

Take a recent Robin Hood grant to place a mental health clinic in a middle school. The idea is to cut down disruption of a student's academic day every time he or she needs to visit a mental health counselor. Robin

Hood had no data on which to base an estimate of the impact of the clinics on future graduation rates from high school. But it did have concurrent data on the percentage of students at this middle school and others who perform on grade level on standardized tests. Relying on outside consultants, Robin Hood settled on the following estimate: For every increase of one standard deviation in raw scores on standardized tests, a student's expected future earnings increase by an average of $2,000 a year. The metrics equation for an in-school mental health clinic would mirror Equation 1, with, among other changes, $2,000 substituting for $6,500.

## Intervention 2: The Value of Staying in College

As a second example of monetizing individual outcomes, consider a grant to provide financial counselors to community college students. Single Stop USA, a Robin Hood grantee, provides such counselors. Surveys show that financial problems force many students to drop out of college short of earning their degrees. The idea of Single Stop is to resolve these financial problems before they do permanent damage.

Here are the building blocks for Robin Hood's metric:

• Research provides rough estimates of the benefit that financial aid can have on dropout rates. One study indicates that a $1,000 increase in financial aid boosts college enrollment or retention by about four percentage points.[2]

• Single Stop USA serves more than 100,000 New Yorkers a year at more than 80 sites around the city. Those sites include every community college campus in the city. At the sites, Single Stop offers visitors, without charge, financial counselors (to handle debt problems and bankruptcy); tax preparers (to help working students apply for tax rebates); lawyers (to appeal government decisions to deny the students food stamps or other entitlements or appeal eviction notices, fight custody battles, and tackle other legal issues); and social workers (to provide general counseling).

• Single Stop USA's community college sites help students create financial cushions. For those students who qualify for any benefits at all, Single Stop connects them to an average of $2,500 in cash and in-kind benefits. (Note: The $2,500 figure cannot be used carelessly. For example, it might not apply to visitors of an expanded program: The next 1,000 visitors might not qualify for as many unclaimed public programs as the previous 1,000 visitors.)

- Data on New York City's community college students shows that about 65 percent of freshman entering two-year colleges that are part of the CUNY (City University of New York) system complete at least one year even without the benefit of financial counseling.[3]

- Research suggests that "some college" can boost the annual earnings of students with demographic characteristics similar to those served by Robin Hood's grantees by perhaps $5,000 a year (beyond what they would have earned had they merely graduated high school). For one year of college, we adopt an estimate of $2,500 for the annual wage boost.[4]

Thus, the benefit of providing financial counseling to community college students can be estimated as follows:

##: *Observed* number of participants in Single Stop community college financial counseling = 300

AA: *Observed* average financial gain to a student visiting a Single Stop site on a community college campus = $2,500.

BB: *Estimated* additional percentage of students who complete at least one more year of college because of an increase in financial reserves = 4 percentage point/$1,000 (based on research);

CC: *Estimated* impact on annual earnings of remaining enrolled in college for an additional year = $2,500.

DD: *Estimated* number of years that college attendance boosts earnings, taken to be 20 in the absence of high-quality information.

Poverty-Fighting Benefit of Increasing College Retention with Financial Counseling:

PDV of: [## × AA × BB × DD]

PDV of [300 × $2,500 × 0.04/$1,000 × $2,500 × 20] = $1.14 million

Having provided examples of assigning mission-related value to single-outcome interventions, we move in the next chapter to examples of assigning value to interventions, perhaps by way of grants, that generate multiple outcomes.

# 7

# Examples of Metrics by Grant: Multi-Outcome Interventions

Chapter 6 assigned a single monetary value to individual outcomes. This chapter extends the framework by monetizing combinations of outcomes, the type of combinations that grants routinely generate. That's why we call this chapter metrics by grant.[1]

Let's review the distinction between a grant that generates a single outcome and a grant that generates multiple outcomes, which is frequent in practice. Recall the example from chapter 1 of a grant to a middle school that covers the cost of providing psychological services for the purpose of helping more students earn their high school diplomas. So far, this is a single-outcome grant. Its metrics capture the extent to which the psychological services boost graduation and, therefore, the future earnings and health of the students. So far, the metrics for the one outcome amounts to the metrics for the grant.

Now let the funder add money to create a college retention service that helps the former middle school students to succeed once they are in college. Note that the funder's metrics need to take account of college persistence because the outcome is relevant to the funder's mission. Studies show that every extra year a student spends in college adds to future earnings. To capture the impact of a grant that generates two outcomes, funders must add together the impact of extra high school graduates and the impact of each additional year of college those graduates complete. What about outcomes that are not relevant to the funder's mission? For the purpose of metrics, they are to be ignored. As we've noted all along, the mission of the grantee routinely overlaps that of the grantor, but the two missions are rarely identical. The grantee will embrace outcomes that the grantor will not, and vice versa.

The following section provides two examples of metrics of multi-outcome grants. We limit our examples to fighting poverty. By the end of this chapter, we'll have dealt with the basic mechanics of assigning monetary value to grants—the basic mechanics of estimating the numerator of a grant's benefit/cost ratio. We'll catch up to the denominator in chapter 8.

## Example 1. Emergency Food Program

Emergency food programs come in two forms. Soup kitchens serve hot meals onsite. Food pantries resemble supermarkets. Either way, food programs attract very poor individuals.

The emergency food programs funded by Robin Hood do a lot more than distribute free food. Said another way, the programs aim for many different outcomes. The sites screen visitors to determine who's eligible for government-funded entitlement programs (like food stamps, Medicaid, federal disability payments, veteran's benefits, and housing subsidies), and enroll those who are determined to be eligible. The sites provide free financial counselors to solve clients' debt problems, lawyers to resolve civil disputes, tax preparers to help low-paid workers file for tax refunds, and social workers to help solve substance abuse problems. Robin Hood currently holds food sites accountable for generating 27 outcomes.

The arithmetic associated with Relentless Monetization (RM) grows long and detailed. RM calls for assigning a dollar value to the gains in each of the 27 distinct outcome categories by estimating the difference between its postintervention value and its counterfactual value. Toward that calculation, RM requires answers to questions such as the following: Would visitors to the food site have gone without ample food in the absence of the funder's intervention? In the absence of the funder's intervention, would visitors merely have sought out some other emergency food site for help? Would visitors have found some other means by which to enroll in Medicaid and other government-funded entitlements if the funder had not intervened?

Once the funder has answered these and other pertinent questions, it can then monetize the average value of the improvement in each distinct outcome for the affected individuals. The next step, as shown in chapter 3, is to multiply the number of affected individuals by the average amount by which outcomes improved for them (relative to counterfactual estimates). That multiplication yields an estimate for the value of the gain in each outcome category under review. The funder repeats the calculation for each outcome produced by its intervention and aggregates the outcomes-specific values into a grand total (correcting for double counting wherever possible). The arithmetic, which we laid out schematically as part of the seven-step overview in chapter 1, is presented in the following in more detail for two hypothetical examples and is also available in detail on the Robin Hood Web site.

Where do the numbers on which the arithmetic is based originate? Funders rely first and foremost on data provided by grantees. Take soup kitchens. Funders need data that the funder can readily observe, such as how many meals the soup kitchen provides.

Funders also need data that cannot be observed—counterfactual data, such as how many meals the soup kitchen would have distributed without the help of the funder or how much money visitors to it save because they don't have to buy some of their meals on their own. In some instances, grantees are positioned to provide information germane to estimating counterfactual figures. A soup kitchen, for example, might well survey visitors to document their eating habits before they began taking advantage of free food.

Finally, in those instances in which grantees are not well positioned to provide counterfactual data—for example, data on the long-term health impact of well-balanced meals. In those instances, funders need to dig up the information on their own. RM imposes a demanding, data-driven regimen for grantees and grantor. Robin Hood aims to cover the financial cost of data gathering by its grantees. In any case, the call on staff time and energy is considerable. A grantee's contract with Robin Hood can obligate the grantee to report at year's end on dozens of variables. Then the grantee's and Robin Hood's staffs pore over the numbers. (Robin Hood rarely asks grantees to analyze the information, which is a task it reserves for its own staff, although other funders handle data matters differently.) Given the complexity of the services and the often threadbare administrative capacity of nonprofits, the numbers can be confusing and incomplete. More discussion. More data collection. More data analysis. By the way, in Robin Hood's case, outright fraud appears to be rare, according to surprise audits of its grantees.

Here is an abbreviated list of the benefits that Robin Hood tracks for its emergency food grants.

1. Budget relief

   • Visitors save an estimated $5 per meal (based on data collected by Robin Hood's grantees) by coming to emergency food centers for food rather than purchasing food. The savings can be used to buy some of life's other necessities.

   Thus, [observed # meals served] × [percent of meals that would not be served but for Robin Hood's grant] × [$5 estimated savings per meal]

   Note that the number of meals served is an observed fact as reported to Robin Hood by its grantees; the counterfactual figure for the number of meals comes from an informed guess made by Robin Hood's staff after taking account, for example, of the likelihood that another philanthropic donor would step in were Robin Hood to withdraw; and the $5 figure comes from published surveys of New York City, including by Robin Hood grantees. See Robin Hood's Web site for details.

   PLUS

2. Enrollment in government-subsidized entitlement programs

   RM calls for estimating how many households the funder helps enroll in each entitlement program and, from that number, subtracting the number of households that would likely have enrolled even without the funder's help. Some examples:

   • Food stamps, which average $1,500 per individual, for visitors to Robin Hood's grantees who would not have enrolled without Robin Hood's help.

   Thus, [# new recipients] × [percent of recipients receiving food stamps solely because of Robin Hood's grant] × [$1,500 average value of food stamps per recipient]

   PLUS

   • Medicaid enrollments, whose value is estimated from an external expert's estimate of the improved health status, as measured in quality adjusted life years (QALYs), that accompanies health insurance.

   Thus, [# new recipients] × [percent of recipients receiving Medicaid benefits solely because of Robin Hood's grant] × [0.16 QALY increase, based on external expert's recommendation] × [$50,000 per QALY, as previously explained]

PLUS

- Federal disability payments (Social Security Supplementary Security Income/Social Security Disability), using the same formula as for the previous entitlements but using an average value of $8,500 (based on data provided by grantees)

PLUS

- Cash assistance, using the same formula as for the previous entitlements but using an average value of $4,000 per individual (based on data from Robin Hood's grantees)

PLUS

3. Legal services

For legal services provided at emergency food sites, Robin Hood estimates how many households receive legal counsel only because of Robin Hood's grant and how many more of them win their cases than would have won had they received no help from Robin Hood. With those estimates in hand, Robin Hood proceeds to monetize the value of the separate legal services. Some examples:

- Avoid eviction for a single adult: $10,000
- Avoid eviction of a family with dependents: $30,000
- Gain work authorization for undocumented immigrants: $6,000
- Gain eligibility for unemployment insurance: $6,000
- Bankruptcy filing: $3,500

Behind each estimate lie assumptions and guesswork. Take bankruptcy filing. The benefit of a timely filing includes the amount of debt that gets discharged (beyond the amount that the debtors would have been able to repay on their own); protection against garnishment of wages; increased probably of employment; decreased probability of eviction; and improved credit scores.

PLUS

4. Nonlegal services

- Housing stability (eviction prevention)

Housing stability for low-income households ranks high by nearly anyone's calculus of well-being. Monetizing the value of programs that help households avoid eviction depends on research that tracks the impact of housing instability on physical and mental health; juvenile delinquency; and foster care placements (as reflected by the impact of foster care placement on future earnings).

- Clothing ($14/visitor)
- Dental services (including impacts on earnings and discomfort, measured in QALYs) (0.4 QALY)
- Haircuts ($5 each)
- Showers ($10 each)
- Laundry service ($2.75/load)
- Mailboxes ($18/box)
- Voicemail ($60/line)

It might strike the reader as picayune to list clothing, let alone haircuts and showers. But if the funder sets no value on showers and haircuts, then surely no program officer will include them in the site's grant even if a close accounting would show that the benefits of these services well exceed their costs. The lesson is straightforward: What doesn't get counted won't get funded. The decision to provide showers should be informed by calculation, not wholly determined by assumption.

PLUS

5. Nutrition. Meals distributed by emergency food programs funded by Robin Hood centers generally provide more nutritional value than do meals that visitors consume on their own. There is sketchy evidence of the impact of nutrition on health based on self-reported measures of "food insecurity" and QALYs that researchers have applied to nutritional counseling.

MINUS

6. Correction for possible double counting. The 27 poverty-related benefits that Robin Hood tracks for its food grantees might overlap, creating the risk that some benefits are counted more than once. Robin Hood sometimes cuts the estimated monetized value of a multi-benefit grant by 10 percent or so (a 10 percent "haircut") to ameliorate the problem of such double counting.

On rare occasions, funders have recourse to sophisticated research that teases out the distinct, nonoverlapping impact of separate interventions. But often, on the basis of social science literature, the funder is left with a presumption of double counting but no evidence-based means of gauging the quantitative extent. Here, funders have three options. First, they can wait for experimental research—research that carefully distinguishes the impact of one factor from another—to emerge. Second, funders can undertake expensive experimental research on their own (as Robin Hood is doing in partnership with MDRC, running randomized controlled trials of early childhood interventions). Third, as in this hypothetical example, the funder can make a crude, transparent correction and invite experts to offer better ideas. (See discussion of double counting in chapter 3.)

The one-by-one recitation of benefits may appear numbing, but fixating on details achieves a virtue that is otherwise impossible: transparency.

Take Robin Hood's estimate for the impact of eviction prevention on mental illness. It takes note of the findings of The National Center for Family Homelessness and the Family Housing Fund that almost 20 percent of poor children who are not homeless suffer from mood disorders, but nearly 50 percent of children who are homeless suffer mood disorders. An intervention to prevent homelessness—so-called eviction prevention programs—won't close the entire 30 percentage-point gap. But the funder can reasonably assume that eviction prevention does close a substantial part of the gap. Robin Hood's calculation assumes that relief of depression, based on the Cost-Effectiveness Analysis Registry, raises the health status of children by 0.5 QALY and the impact is approximately the same for adults. These assumptions are not based on randomized controlled trials (RCTs) or any other structured experiment. They are rough cut at best. The point here is that if a reviewer cringes at the 50, 20, or other figures, there's a simple remedy: Cough up evidence for different numbers.

### Example 2. Microlending

Robin Hood funds loans to low-income individuals who seek to set up home businesses or startup ventures such as hair cutting operations, selling cosmetics, resale of imported trinkets, or other small-scale activities. The idea is to raise household income.

For purpose of metrics, it tracks the following items:

- Extra *net* earnings of borrowers, taking due account of the failure rate of startup businesses and the borrower's possible withdrawal from labor market

- Extra earnings of poor workers hired by the borrower
- Savings on interest payments on loans (compared with rates that borrowers would otherwise have to pay to loan sharks or credit cards)
- Interest on additional savings, if the microlending program requires borrowers to hit a savings target
- Improved credit score of borrowers with successful loan repayment, leading to, for example: small security deposits on purchaser of cell phones and the like; for veterans, national security clearance; less expensive ways to handle adverse economic shocks
- Educational value to borrower from starting a business (for example, some owners receive one semester of college credit for having run a business)

RM calls on funders to track outcomes, such as those in the preceding list, of those who take out microloans from their grantees. The next step is to compare those actual outcomes with counterfactual outcomes. What level of earnings, hires, savings, credit scores, and business savvy would the microborrowers have achieved had they not had the benefit of the microloans? Some microborrowers, absent the funder's grant, would have abandoned the idea of starting a home business. Some microborrowers, absent the funder's grant, would have started their businesses with the help of another microlender, a loan shark, or by tapping their credit line with a local bank. Most important, some microborrowers will have to drop out of the labor force in order to run their startup business, bringing the net earnings of the new enterprise below its gross earnings. The funder needs to account for all of these interactions in estimating counterfactual earnings and, therefore, estimating the monetized value of the microloans.

For microloans, Robin Hood so far has based metrics of microlending on crude estimates of the borrower's counterfactual earnings. But it is about to undertake a multiyear randomized control trial (RCT) of one of its microlenders. The rationale for taking up the expensive study is threefold.

First, the lure of microlending to a poverty fighting funder is powerful. Microlending is, at least in theory, readily replicable. If a well-defined model can be proved successful, microlending could transform the business of fighting poverty.

Second, the literature on microlending is mixed. The research community simply does not know if it can be made to work in poor neighborhoods of otherwise wealthy countries. The best-executed studies have, in general, found small impacts. The carefully executed studies have mostly been conducted in very poor countries, shedding unreliable light on microlending's potential in urban America. And most studies have tracked microborrowers for relatively short periods, giving an unreliable indication of long-term impacts. Pinning down the impact of any model of microlending requires a serious, and no doubt costly, undertaking.

Third, better done studies suggest that creating a carefully crafted control group is essential to accurate assessment. In the absence of an RCT, the obvious and easiest choice for estimating counterfactual success among microborrowers would be to use baseline data—pre-loan levels of success. But baseline data do not inspire confidence in this context. Many of the applicants for microloans have hit rock bottom economically, and their decision to apply for a microloan reflects a commitment to turn around their economic fortunes. If their application for a microloan is denied, that commitment may well drive them to find some other way to escape poverty. The best guess of their future success is higher than their baseline earnings. How much higher? In the absence of an RCT to answer the question, Robin Hood assumes that counterfactual earnings of microborrowers—their earnings had they not received microloans—would have risen half as much as their earnings actually did rise once they received microloans. Although Robin Hood has lots of reasons to conclude that the 50 percent assumption is reasonable, it is far from certain. To its credit, however, the assumption is explicit and critics can substitute their own judgments.

This and the previous chapter outlined the process for assigning a single monetized value to an intervention—perhaps delivered by way of a grant—that generates multiple benefits. The next chapter completes the exercise of RM by taking account of costs and estimating all-important benefit/cost ratios.

# 8

# Completing the Analytical Traverse: Small-Bore Benefit/Cost Analysis

Over the past several chapters, we described the all-important process of monetizing interventions. Now we complete the analytical traverse that we call Relentless Monetization (RM), showing how to use the estimates to make smart philanthropic decisions.

Specifically, this chapter explores the use of benefit/cost ratios to rank the relative impacts of philanthropic interventions—what we call small-bore benefit/cost analysis. The ratios capture the collective mission-related benefit that individual grants create per dollar cost to the funder. In the case of Robin Hood, benefit/cost ratios capture the extent to which a particular grant raises the collective living standards of poor New Yorkers per dollar cost to Robin Hood.

Small-bore benefit/cost ratios move philanthropic measures of success closer to those used by commercial enterprises, echoing the clarity and consistency of commercial rates of return. And just as commercial rates of return allow for comparing business enterprises of all forms and purposes, small-bore benefit/cost ratios allow for comparing philanthropic interventions of all forms and purposes. The upshot is that small-bore benefit/cost analysis provides nonprofits a tool by which to achieve consistently powerful outcomes, and it does so in a way that gives donors clear evidence (good or bad) about the impact of their money. It is no surprise, then, that Robin Hood's financially savvy donors embraced the rigor of RM early.

## The Arithmetic of Small-Bore Benefit/Cost Analysis

RM calls on funders to estimate benefit/cost ratios for proposed or actual interventions or grants. (We use the two words interchangeably here.)

For the sake of simplicity, assume the funder bases grant decisions solely on the basis of the quantitative measures that underlie benefit/cost calculations. Further, assume for the moment that a grant's benefit/cost ratio remains constant as modest amounts of money are added or subtracted. Later in this chapter we consider when it is or is not wise to make this assumption in practice.

The numerator of the benefit/cost ratio captures the aggregate benefit, as defined by the funder's mission, created by the intervention. The examples presented in chapters 6 and 7 show how a funder can go about estimating that number. For the denominator, the funder can more often than not simply plug in the cash outlay on a grant (the size of the grant). The denominator becomes more complicated if the funder provides grantees resources other than cash, another issue we will address later in the chapter. The ratio captures the funder's best estimate of the mission-driven benefits created by a grant *per dollar* of costs.

Benefit/cost ratios provide guidance for funders who want to spend money where it does the most mission-relevant good. Take the case of a job training program funded by Robin Hood. Assume it generates only one benefit, higher earnings. Assuming that the benefit/cost ratio stays constant as dollars are added or subtracted, a ratio of 5:1 means that Robin Hood boosts the current and future incomes of poor New Yorkers by $5 for every $1 it spends on the program. The numerator for other types of programs that Robin Hood funds may be interpreted similarly. No matter what the nature of the program, as long as its purpose is to fight poverty, the benefit/cost ratio captures the rise in living standards per dollar spent by the funder. Funders can use their estimated benefit/cost ratios for various projects to compare the impact of one project with another no matter how the two projects differ in their approach to accomplishing the funder's mission.

As such, benefit/cost ratios provide invaluable information by which to decide whether any particular grant is the wisest possible use of the funder's money. Once benefit/cost ratios are estimated for projects under review, staff can shift funds from programs with low benefit/cost ratios to those with high benefit/cost ratios. Assume, for simplicity, that Programs A and B are both job training programs and shifting a modest amount of money back and forth between the two programs won't change their respective benefit/cost ratios. Assume that the benefit/cost ratio of Program A is 10:1 and that of Program B is 8:1. Reducing B's grant by $1 reduces the earnings of poor New Yorkers by an estimated $8. Transferring that same $1 to Program A raises the earnings of poor New Yorkers by an estimated $10. Thus, the mere transfer of $1 to Program A from Program B raises the earnings of poor New Yorkers by an estimated $10 − $8 = $2. This $2 increase in earnings is accomplished without the funder spending one extra dime. RM ensures that the funder spends smarter, not necessarily more.

Spending smarter in this way, say by shifting resources from a jobs training program with a lower benefit/cost ratio to a similar program with a higher ratio, can yield big dividends. But the real power of RM comes into prominent display once we drop the simplifying assumption that all programs are of the same type. Again, let's use Robin Hood as an example. Its mission is to improve the living standards of poor New Yorkers, where living standards are comprised of income and a monetized value of health status. Using small-bore benefit/cost analysis, Robin Hood can track and compare the impact of any and all interventions, whether they involve job training, early childhood interventions, microloans, housing for the homeless, health initiatives, or any other poverty-fighting activities. Suppose Program C, whatever its composition, generates a 20:1 benefit/cost ratio; that is, raises or lowers the collective living standards of poor New Yorkers by $20 for every $1 spent or withdrawn from Program C. And suppose Program D, whatever its composition, generates a 2:1 benefit/cost ratio, it raises or changes benefits for poor New Yorkers by $2 for every extra $1 spent or withdrawn. This means that transferring $1 from Program D, whatever it is, to Program C, whatever it is, raises living standards of poor New Yorkers by $18 (= $20 − $2) for the same money.

## Refining the Arithmetic

In the preceding discussion, we assumed that benefit/cost ratios remain constant as modest amounts of money are transferred to and fro. That simplified the exposition without distorting important lessons. Here we look briefly at how the funder would need to proceed when life's more complicated.

Let's assume that each successive block of funding ($10,000, $100,000, $1 million—the exact amount does not matter)—that a funder allocates to a particular intervention yields a smaller bump to benefits than did the previous block of funding. If so, then benefit/cost ratios move up and down as a funder moves money in and out of a specific intervention. Let's further assume that the funder faces an investment opportunity that's lumpy: The funder can either make a large investment in the project or none at all. It cannot titrate the size of its investment. Under these assumptions, how should the funder make the correct investment decision?

Here's a specific thought experiment.

The funder is faced with the option to make job training grants in million dollar tranches. With the first $1 million, the job training program generates benefits (in the form of future earnings increases) of $5 for every one of those first million dollars that the funder spends. But if the funder adds a second $1 million tranche, the program may not generate another $5 million of benefits. Perhaps the additional instructors who would have to be hired to double the size of the program would not be as effective as the first set of instructors. Perhaps the jobs that additional graduates will find will not pay as much as the existing jobs. And so on. Bottom line: the first $1 million tranche generates $5 of benefits for every dollar spent. But the second $1 million tranche may generate only $3 of benefits for every dollar spent. Let's note that once the two tranches are spent—once the funder spends $2 million—the overall (average) benefit/cost ratio is 4:1.

As introductory economics students recognize, we're rehearsing the difference between average impact and marginal impact. The average benefit/cost ratio of a $2 million grant is 4:1, which is the average of the benefit/cost ratio from the first tranche (5:1) and second tranche (3:1). Whether the funder should make the first million dollar grant depends on whether it has other grant opportunities that will generate more than $5 of benefits per dollar. But whether the funder should make the second million dollar grant depends on whether it has other grant opportunities that generate more than a 3:1 benefit/cost ratio. Said another way, the average benefit/cost ratio of 4:1 on a $2 million grant is irrelevant to either decision. The important point is that the funder, faced with a declining benefit/cost ratio, will likely invest less in the project than would be the case if the benefit/cost ratio would remain high (at 5:1) despite the size of funder's investments. Here, the funder may well find that the first tranche makes sense at 5:1, but the second tranche, at 3:1, does not make good sense because the funder has better opportunities elsewhere.

Let's change the example to make a different analytical point. Assume that a funder has $10 million, and no more, to spend, and faces only three options for spending its funds, Program L, Program M, and Program N, among which it must choose. We assume that the projects are "lumpy," in the sense that investments must be of a particular size, neither more nor less.

> Program L: This program has a benefit/cost ratio of 10:1. The project can be scaled neither down nor up. Funding Program L involves a minimum outlay of $8 million and yields a net benefit of $72 (= $80 – $8) million.
>
> Program M: This program has a benefit/cost ratio of 9:1. It requires a minimum investment of $5.5 million and yields a net benefit of $44 (= $49.5 – $5.5) million.
>
> Program N: This program has a benefit/cost ratio of 8:1. It requires a minimum investment of $4.5 million and yields a net benefit of $31.5 (= $36 – $4.5) million (Table 8.1)

Consider some options. Option 1: spend $10 million on Program L. Option 2: spend $10 million on a combination of Programs M and N. Given its $10 million budget and these three choices, the funder ought to choose Option 2 over Option 1. Although the two options cost the same, the combination of Programs M and N generate a combined benefit of $75.5 million, above the net benefit of $72 million that Program L generates. Note the superiority of Option 2, even though the benefit/cost ratios of Programs M and N fall short of that for Program L (9:1 and 8:1, respectively, vs. 10:1 for Program L).

What distinguishes this thought experiment from those presented earlier in this book is that until now we've assumed that funders could pour money into the program with the highest benefit/cost ratio without driving

Table 8.1

| Program L | | Program M | | Program N | |
|-----------|-----------|-----------|-----------|-----------|-----------|
| Funding | B/C Ratio | Funding | B/C Ratio | Funding | B/C Ratio |
| $8,000,000 | 10 to 1 | $5,500,000 | 9 to 1 | $4,500,000 | 8 to 1 |
| additional $ | 0 | additional $ | 0 | additional $ | 0 |

the ratio lower. In this thought experiment, we ruled out this flexibility by the assumption that the investment options were lumpy.

The exact nature of restrictions on investment opportunities dictates the funder's best response. Suppose, for example, that none of the programs could be scaled up, but all three programs could be scaled down in a way that would hold their benefit/cost ratio constant. Here, Program N would not receive any funding; rather, Program L would be fully funded at $8 million and Program M would be scaled down from $5.5 to $2 million. The total net benefits achieved would be $88 (= $80 + $18 − $8 − $2). Here, in effect, every dollar would be allocated to whatever program yielded the highest benefit/cost ratio.

If the funder were able to scale any given program up without changing its benefit/cost ratio, it would allocate every dollar to whatever use offered the highest benefit/cost ratio, which in turn would yield the highest net benefit. But when benefit/cost ratios cannot be assumed (relatively) constant, or when investment opportunities are lumpy, then the funder needs to make decisions according to the *difference* between total benefits and costs rather than according to the *ratio* of benefit to costs. In this more complicated situation, the funders would need to find the combination of lumpy investments that yields the greatest net benefit while still holding total funding to no more than the maximum available budget. In the preceding example, the funder exhausted its budget by spending on Programs M and N. But in a world of lumpy funding opportunities, the funder may find that it creates the highest net benefit by leaving some of its budget unspent.

The "differences" and "ratios" referred to above are calculated from the exact same two numbers: the numerator and denominator of the benefit/cost ratio. That's mightily important because it means we need not revise previous chapters. The exact same words apply. Same numbers. Same estimations. Same explanations. We chose to develop the ideas behind RM in terms of ratios because it simplified the analysis, making it easier to grasp and apply. We've sacrificed details but not conceptual coherence.

The reader may well wonder which assumption is more realistic: Can a funder pour more money into a project and assume that expansion won't drive benefit/cost ratios lower? Or do funders face falling ratios as they rapidly expand programs? In Robin Hood's case, the answer appears to be that modest expansions can be accomplished without driving benefit/cost ratios down. But replication or other forms of massive expansion often do drive measures of success down.

Indeed, that's the reason Robin Hood makes more than 200 grants a year to allocate its $120 million grant making budget. That's a large number of grants. The question naturally arises, should Robin Hood replicate its superstar performers, raising their grants twofold, fourfold, or even more, and cutting out grantees that don't qualify as superstars? The idea holds out the dual promise of raising Robin Hood's average benefit/cost ratio and, by cutting out grants, reduce the need to hire staff.

The idea might sound tantalizing. But when a team of pro bono consultants from McKinsey, the world renowned consulting firm, and staffers from Robin Hood tried to come up with candidates for massive replication/ scaling, they found none. Why not? First, Robin Hood's program officers, like those of many other funders, look hard for opportunities to replicate or "scale" superstars. The fact that there were no obvious missed opportunities should not be wholly surprising. Second, consider the details. Every plan to replicate raises torrents of fact laden issues. Take a program that Robin Hood funds at one location in Brooklyn to train chronically unemployed women to drive commercial trucks. It racks up spectacular results. (The women drivers earn impressive salaries.) Why not replicate the program in the other boroughs? The answer is the economics of a single market. Newly trained drivers, no matter from what borough they emerge, enter a single regional labor market. There's simply no large unrequited demand for commercial truck drivers in New York City. Replicating the training program in other boroughs would drive up the number of job seekers, but do nothing to drive up the number of hires. The current gaudy benefit/cost ratio would come tumbling down. Details. Details.

## Monetizing Costs: Benefits "Here" Versus Benefits "There"

The previous chapters have riveted on assessing benefits. Here we dwell, however briefly, on costs. In general, estimating costs is far more straight-forward than estimating benefits.

If a funder makes a cash grant of $1 million to XYZ, then its costs are, at the risk of belaboring the obvious, $1 million. The funder has $1 million less to give to some other philanthropic endeavor.

The matter gets more complicated if the funder provides grantees non-cash resources. Take technical assistance. Let's suppose the funder arranges for a commercial consulting firm to provide strategic advice to XYZ. There are three options.

First, a consulting firm provides the advice as one of a limited number of pro bono projects. Because the funder pays nothing, it will be tempted to regard the projects as costless. Not so quick. In this case, by assumption, asking the consultant to serve XYZ means that the consultant will not serve some other grantee, RST, free. Thus, the cost of serving XYZ is the value of benefits that the consultant could have created had it served RST rather than XYZ.

Second, a consulting firm provides the advice pro bono, but it does not reduce the number of other projects it will service without charge. (Said another way, the number of consulting projects offered without charge is, in effect, unlimited.) Under this assumption, the cost of the advice, as viewed by the funder, is truly zero.

Third, the funder pays the consulting firm a fee for its advice. In this case, the advice merely adds to the out-of-pocket costs of the underlying grant.

Perhaps here is a good point at which to review the economist's fundamental logic of measuring costs as part of benefit/cost analysis. Take a funder that mulls funding Program A or Program B, the next best alternative. The standard way of expressing economic logic is to say, "fund Program A if its *benefits* exceed its *costs*." But what economists really mean by this instruction is to fund Program A if the *benefits* it generates exceed the *benefits* that Program B generates with the same amount of money. In other words, the benefit/cost framework of modern economics appears to noneconomists to be comparing benefits to costs. But what the framework actually does is compare "benefits here" (the program under review) to "benefits there" (the benefits that could be achieved by putting the money to the best alternative use). The reader might find the imperative to compare benefits to benefits clearer than the imperative to compare benefits to costs (which sounds a bit like comparing apples to oranges). Whatever the terminology, the imperative is the same: Fund Program A if there is no Program B that generates more benefit with the same amount of money. And don't fund Program A if there is a Program B that generates more benefit with the same amount of money.

The generalization of the previous point is that funders need to take into account the full cost (in economist speak, the "opportunity costs") of any resources it devotes toward an intervention, cash or noncash. And the best way to think about opportunity cost is to think of benefits. The opportunity cost of providing resources to Program A is the benefit that the funder could have generated had it devoted the resources instead to the best alternative use of the funds.

## Why "Small-Bore"?

We call the outlined steps "small-bore" benefit/cost analysis because of its application to the individual, often small, components of grants made to single grantees by a single funder. Contrast that use of benefit/cost analysis to its more familiar use, as a workhorse of modern economics in the analysis of major public works projects like dams, highways, and public health programs. Let's call this large-bore benefit/cost analysis, which is often required under specific pieces of legislation (like some environmental protection laws) and federal, state, and local administrative rules and procedures. Small-bore benefit/cost analysis fixates on details, which makes good sense given its application to small and modest sized grants. Large-bore benefit/ cost analysis, given its application to public works projects, routinely overlooks many of the details that preoccupy its small-bore cousin (as set forth in chapters 6 and 7). Another difference between small- and large-bore benefit/cost analyses concerns data. Public works projects often generate tons of relevant data. By contrast, small-bore benefit/cost analysis often works with little more than morsels of useful data. Finally, large-bore benefit/cost analysis is commonplace in the public works arena. Small-bore benefit/cost analysis barely exists in the philanthropic arena.

## Confusing Inputs for Outcomes

An agency of the New York City government plans to post a "scorecard" of performance measures for nonprofits with which it does business. The scorecard will focus on readily measurable variables, like cost per enrollee for city subsidized job training programs.

It's a scorecard. But it's not the right scorecard.

Performance is validly measured by considering benefits and costs (benefits per dollar of cost). Focusing on only benefits or only costs is dead wrong, and will drive private and public funders in all the wrong directions.

For starters, ask yourself which figure is better: high per-enrollee cost (say $5,000 per enrollee) or low per-enrollee cost (say, $2,500). The answer is: You can't tell without additional information. The issue is not whether a nonprofit spends a lot of money. The issue is whether the nonprofit achieves a lot of benefits per dollar spent. To say the obvious, incurring high costs is worse than incurring low costs if both produce the same outcomes. But if high costs reflect the fact that the nonprofit is going after more disadvantaged enrollees—enrollee that are more costly to serve—then high costs may be a terrific investment. The issue is whether the high costs are the means for achieving even higher benefits. If the city's scorecard blindly steers funders to low-cost nonprofits, it may do unspeakable damage by driving public and private money to nonprofits that provide the least effective programs or serve the least needy (and therefore least expensive to serve) individuals.

Smart philanthropy, whether practicing RM or some other evidence-based strategy, balances benefits and costs. A scorecard that purports to rank nonprofits has two and only two choices. It can limit itself to comparing identical nonprofits: same mission, same clientele, same outcomes, same region. Under that option, the scorecard does nearly nothing because no nonprofits share all such characteristics. Or the scorecard can compare nonidentical nonprofits. But to do that requires: first, taking outcomes (in other words, benefits) into account; second, taking nonidentical outcomes into account; and, therefore, third, monetizing outcomes so as to compare benefit/cost figures for the nonprofits under scrutiny. Taking shortcuts—posting what's easy to measure across nonprofits, like cost per enrollee—invites wrong, reckless inferences. Responsible funders do not fixate on benefits to the exclusion of costs, nor do they fixate on costs to the exclusion of benefits. Responsible funders balance benefits and costs. Enter Relentless Monetization.

# 9

# Key Generalities: Q&A

The previous chapters demonstrated the ability of Relentless Monetization (RM) to drive funders toward smart, often nonobvious decisions. This chapter draws out key generalities by answering questions often posed by funders, donors, and nonprofits seeking funders and donors.

1. *For funders who choose to practice RM, are benefit/cost ratios the sole basis for making grants?*

No. No. A thousand times no.

The ratios are useful guides, but they are imprecise. They amount to one of several tools in a funder's tool kit. Smart funders would no more make grant decisions based solely on the arithmetic of benefit/cost ratios than smart admissions officers at competitive undergraduate colleges would make admissions decisions based solely on the arithmetic of SAT scores. SAT scores provide important information. Along with other information—like letters of recommendation and high school course grades—test scores steer admission decisions toward candidates with the best chance to succeed. Similarly, benefit/cost ratios provide important information. Along with other information, benefit/cost ratios steer a funder toward grantees with the best chance to fulfill its mission. Smart program officers base grant decisions on evidence that goes well beyond the information that can be reasonably captured by a benefit/cost estimate. It matters if the grantee relies on one aging charismatic leader who refuses to prepare for succession. It matters if the grantee's current corps of private and public donors appears fickle.

What does a funder do if the arithmetic doesn't square with compelling qualitative evidence?

Take a former grantee of Robin Hood's, a provider of permanent housing for formerly homeless families. Giving homeless families permanent shelter surely fights poverty. And Robin Hood's staff knew the particular residence its grant supported ranked among the best—if not *the* best—in New York. The 60 or so families lived in beautiful quarters. And none returned to the street. Yet when staff estimated at the grantee's benefit/cost ratio, it ranked at the bottom of Robin Hood's list. Staff "knew" the program was stellar. But the number said the opposite.

Staff's first thought was that the monetization of this grant may have overlooked some of the program's poverty-fighting benefit. Staff asked, did the congregate care facility do more than provide a roof over the residents' heads? It might be training residents to hold jobs outside the residence. It might be providing dental and other types of medical care that the residents would not otherwise receive. If so, the answer is to identify and monetize. And what if congregate care fulfills Robin Hood's mission in ways Robin Hood so far omits, like giving the formerly homeless residents a sense of physical and emotional safety? Robin Hood, as pointed out previously, does not yet count safety as a mission-relevant benefit.

That said, staff came increasingly to a different conclusion. Perhaps what staff thought it knew just wasn't true. The residence does great things, but their total value per dollar does not stack up against other ways that Robin Hood fights poverty. In the case of permanent housing, Robin Hood faced the need to spend tens of thousands of dollars per family on the same families year after year after year. Remember: The housing is successfully permanent. The families stay put. The residence may well achieve *its* mission of keeping formerly homeless families off the streets. But Robin Hood may have more productive uses of its money. For example, Robin Hood spends equivalent amounts (thousands of dollars per year) on job training or schools. But in those cases, the identity of the individuals changes each year. Robin Hood lifts new individuals out of poverty each year. The fact that a stellar permanent housing facility might not rank high begins to make good poverty-fighting sense. At the very least, the question warranted investigation.

Indeed, Robin Hood's staff took several years to reconcile qualitative and quantitative evidence. The seemingly low benefit/cost ratio was treated as a signal to intensively investigate, a signal to diagnose the issue. After searching in vain for important benefits that its metrics so far overlooked, Robin Hood's staff followed the lead of its quantitative measures and cut back support. (Incidentally, this example highlights another great advantage of RM: Used properly, it offers a way for nonprofits to reduce the paralysis and inefficiency in resource allocation that come from entrenched positions of program staff.)

2. *Does RM trample donor intent?*

Practiced carelessly, that's a danger. In theory, RM implements, not tramples, the preferences and philanthropic intentions of donors. Return to the question in our earlier chapter about saving oysters in the Chesapeake Bay versus polar bears in the Arctic. It's not for a procedure, like RM, to say whether saving the oysters is worth sacrificing, if need be, the life of a single polar bear or the life of every polar bear in the Arctic. That's for donors to say. And, as donors, they bear no burden to ground their preferences in scientific facts. It's the job of RM to match the choices that funders make to their donors' preferences. That's the theory. In practice, RM may tend to select out for concreteness and specificity. As such, it can leave hard-to-quantify benefits in the proverbial lurch. Recall that Robin Hood has given short shrift to safety when monetizing the value of after school and permanent housing programs. The problem is in principle solvable—as shown by the treatment of health, another hard to quantify benefit. The important implication for practitioners of RM is that they need to monetize significant nonpecuniary benefits. It bears repeating that funders cannot avoid quantification if the goal is to rank grants by something other than personal whim. The moment a funder decides what to fund and what not to fund, it has ranked the relative value of its grant opportunities. The funder may not have thought about the rankings. It may not recognize, let alone admit, the rankings it has exercised. But it has ranked nonetheless, just as a family, having allocated its budget, has ranked the value of everything it buys or could afford but did not buy. What distinguishes RM from other ways to make philanthropic decisions is that the routine forces the funder to make its values and preferences transparent. It thereby holds its decisions up to scrutiny by itself and others.

3. *Does pursuing interventions with high benefit/cost ratios drive funders to specialize—to fund one program type to the exclusion of most others?*

In general, no.

Funders relying on benefit/cost calculations would be no more likely to settle on one program type than would consumers weighing pros and cons settle on the same dessert every day. Benefit/cost decisions rarely produce all-or-nothing decisions. The question is not whether a funder winds up choosing only education programs or only job training programs. Rather, the question is how many (and which) education programs do we fund versus how many (and which) job training programs do we fund? That should come as no surprise. Consider the following thought experiment. Imagine a menu of 1,000 programs, of which 600 are related to education and 400 are related to job training. Suppose we can fund 500 programs from among the 1,000. Let's rank the 1,000 programs by their benefit/cost ratios. We would not be shocked if, say, the 10 best programs happened to be education programs. But we surely would be shocked to find that the 500th best education program was ranked higher than any one of the 400 best job training programs. In the real world, the best set of 500 programs will include some from each program type.

Also, benefit/cost ratios are not constants. They change as money is poured into or taken out of operations. Take two job training programs, XXX and YYY. Suppose that the benefit/cost ratio for XXX at last year's level of funding was 5:1 and that for YYY was 4:1. These facts alone do not guarantee that shifting dollars to XXX from YYY will create more total benefits. XXX may not be poised for expansion. Pouring more dollars into XXX might not wind up expanding the number of trainees it successfully places in jobs. And so on. In economist speak, the average benefit produced by XXX exceeds the marginal benefit, by which economists mean the additional benefits that would be generated by adding some additional money to XXX's grant. Said another way, XXX may well be the more successful program on average, but it may well waste any *additional* resources, and thus be the less successful of the two programs on the margin.

4. *Would philanthropists be better served by relying on comparisons of cost-effectiveness, which are far simpler than benefit/cost comparisons?*

Cost-effectiveness comparisons are simple. They tend to fixate on costs and ignore benefits. Funders gravitate toward them because tracking costs is easier than measuring outcomes, especially when outcomes come in hard-to-compare flavors. But funders pay a high price for simplicity. Cost-effectiveness studies are appropriate only under rarefied conditions and dangerous when wrongly applied.

Ask yourself which program is better: one that spends $5,000 per enrollee or one that spends only $2,500 per enrollee. The answer is: Without information about benefit, the question has no answer.

Comparing two programs only on the basis of costs is okay *only* if the programs under comparison produce the exact same outcome. In that case, choosing the cheaper of the two makes complete sense. But if outcomes are not the same, then focusing on costs to the exclusion of benefits produces perverse decisions. Why perverse? Carelessly applied, focusing on costs drives funders away from high-cost interventions. If the interventions are costly because they waste money, avoiding them is good. But if an intervention is costly because it takes a lot of money to provide a sky-high benefit, then the failure to take benefits into account drives funders away from costly to serve participants; that is to say, drives funders away from serving the neediest individuals.

Take two job training programs. If they both serve demographically similar trainees and teach comparable skills, then by all means the funder can rank the two grant-making opportunities solely on the basis of relative costs. But what if one program serves ex-offenders and the other program serves community college graduates. Assume the former face grim employment prospects in the absence of training and the latter face good employment prospects even without further training. Taking these facts into account, the funder might well surmise that counterfactual earnings of ex-offenders fall far short of counterfactual earnings of community college graduates and that the mission-relevant value of helping the former trainees exceeds the value of helping the latter trainees. In this circumstance—a common circumstance, in which counterfactual success differs among programs—basing funding decisions solely on relative costs defies good sense.

Cost-effectiveness is terrific in the rare instance that the funder is faced with programs that produce an identical outcome, a rare instance indeed. Otherwise, responsible funders balance benefits and costs. Enter RM to solve the problem of comparing programs that produce dissimilar outcomes.

We return to cost-effectiveness measures in chapter 11.

5. *Are small-bore benefit/cost estimates accurate?*

Yes and no. The answer depends on what standard of proof applies.

Funders need not, indeed cannot, emulate academics. Academics are obligated to marshal evidence to prove propositions beyond a statistical shadow of a doubt. The obligation is to convince disinterested parties. The academic standard is akin to that which governs criminal trials. But were funders to apply such a standard, grant making would screech to an audible halt. In general, no such fail-safe evidence exists in the social sciences. Funders would make few if any grants, an unacceptable, if not cruel, outcome.

The appropriate standard for funders is akin to that which governs civil trials: proof by a simple preponderance of available evidence. Following that rule, funders make grants for which the evidence in favor outweighs the evidence in favor of making other possible grants. Making decisions on the basis of a simple preponderance of evidence is not as ironclad as "beyond a statistical shadow of a doubt," but it is a far cry from personal whim. And what distinguished RM from other ways to decide grants is the fact that the routine forces the funder to make its values and preferences, as well as the metrics that have guided allocation decisions, both explicit and transparent.

The point of RM is not to base grant making on mathematical or statistical certainties, but to improve upon the informal, intuition-driven and analytically incoherent current practice of typical philanthropies. Said another way, the goal of RM is to improve upon current guesswork, not pretend to achieve theoretical purity.

6. *How do Robin Hood's estimated benefit/cost ratios compare to those found in academic studies of similar kinds of programs?*

In general, they are higher. That raises the question, are the estimates exaggerated? There's no easy answer. But before coming to judgment, consider some reasons to expect Robin Hood's estimates to exceed those of academics.

First and foremost, Robin Hood, as a private philanthropy, funds only the best performing grantees. Research literature usually answers the question: How does the typical grantee operate? Thus, a federal study of early childhood programs might look at a random sample of Head Start sites, whereas Robin Hood would assess only its grantees, the best early childhood sites in New York City.

Second, as a private funder, Robin Hood takes account of only the resources it provides to an intervention. It takes the contributions of public and other private sources as given (unless they are tied to Robin Hood's grant). Robin Hood estimates only the marginal impact of its grant and its grant only. Research literature, by contrast, usually answers questions about the return to *all* of the resources that go into an intervention. Neither is wrong. Their benefit/cost estimates are designed to answer different questions.

Third, many research studies of the type of interventions that Robin Hood funds fixate on earnings only. By incorporating health related outcomes, for example, improvement of health that come with high school graduation, independent of the impact on earnings, Robin Hood will see larger benefits than if it looked at earnings alone.

7. *How does RM deal with risk?*

Answer: In the simplest possible manner, so far.

Virtually any grant poses risks. Projected benefits and cost are just that, projections. Future circumstances will dictate surprises. The grantee's leader might resign. Government contracts might be rescinded. Recession might hit fundraising hard. And so on. A funder's well-recognized gamble might fall short. Here we flag the issue of risk, a topic we will treat at length in chapter 12.

As described so far, RM involves estimating the benefit and cost of a grant with single numbers (so-called point estimates) rather than with a range of numbers. And RM does not weight estimates of benefits and costs by the confidence the funder has in the estimates.

More precisely, the numerator and denominator of benefit/cost ratios reflect expected values in the mathematical sense of weighing possible outcomes by their probabilities of occurrence. What is the probability that that an academic intervention will boost graduation rates by a specified amount? What is the probability that high school graduates will go on to on to earn an extra $6,500 per year (or any other assumed amount) above that earned by their peers who drop out of high school? The bulk of this book, especially chapters 6 and 7, took a "risk-neutral" stance to risk. We used point estimates for the likely impact of grants—in general, by multiplying the likely number of individuals whom a grant helps by the average size of the gain. (For example, an education intervention would be estimated by multiplying the expected number of additional high school graduates and the expected earnings gain for each of those additional graduates.) We have not favored or punished proposals that, given the same expected gain, do so by presenting the funder with risky outcomes (sizeable probabilities of big gains and big losses) or relatively certain outcomes (high probabilities of a respectable outcome).

Take two programs, each creating a certain mission-relevant benefit of $1,000 per successful participant. AAA offers a 100 percent probability of helping 10 individuals. That's an expected gain of $10,000. BBB, by contrast, offers a 50 percent probability of helping 20 individuals (for a gain of $20,000) and a 50 percent chance of helping no one (for a gain of $0). BBB's expected gain is, therefore, $0.5 \times \$20,000 + 0.5 \times 0 = \$10,000$. Under our risk-neutral stance, AAA and BBB would be deemed equally attractive. But funders could reasonably choose otherwise. A funder who dislikes uncertainty might choose AAA rather than BBB. For the same expected outcome, program AAA never disappoints. By contrast, a funder who likes risk—preserving an option of a big gain ($20,000), albeit at the cost of preserving an option of no gain ($0)—might prefer BBB.

One programmatic case warrants special attention. Pilots refer to experiments of innovative ideas. Nearly by definition, pilots are unlikely to succeed because they are high risk. But if they succeed, the now-proven idea may generate huge benefits. Think of a computer program that promises to revolutionize the teaching of language skills to disadvantaged students. We see promises of computerized instruction by the bucketful. Nearly none succeed. But if any one were to succeed, the impact on the most disadvantaged segment of society would be massive. Here, as is typical with proposed pilots, we're dealing with two extreme numbers, neither of which we know with any confidence. We have a small, perhaps extremely small, probability of success. And we have a large, perhaps extremely large, potential gain. Multiplying two extreme numbers, neither of which we know with any confidence, produces a number (expected gain) that warrants little confidence.

We tackle this issue at length in chapter 12.

8. *Are benefit/cost estimates subject to manipulation?*

They sure are. The rules of algebra dictate that making modest changes in numerators and denominators can change ratios hugely. Take a grant for which the funder estimates benefits of $40,000 at costs of $50,000; therefore, a benefit/cost ratio of 0.8. A ratio below 1.0 indicates that the grant does more harm than good (in the economist's sense that the funder could spend the same money elsewhere and do more total good). But jack up the numerator by 15 percent and cut the denominator by 15 percent (to $46,000 and $42,500, respectively) and the benefit/cost ratio rises to 1.1, which might be high enough to warrant funding.

There's simply no denying that fooling with the numbers can produce squirrely, or at least self-serving, answers. The first, and best, antidote to this is transparency. Make the assumptions underlying the metrics both explicit and available for scrutiny. Another helpful approach, here as elsewhere where decisions need be made in the face of uncertainty, is to subject analyses to sensitivity analysis: Substitute various plausible values for benefits and costs and see how the recommendation might change. If it takes only a small (and not unreasonable) change in one of the factors determining benefits (or costs) to change a promising looking grant to something very unpromising, it's a sure signal to exercise some caution and gather better data. And, of course, it is essential that the funder make sure that program staffs—the folks who construct the benefit/cost estimates—are not rewarded for producing gaudy numbers. A more detailed answer would take this book far afield.

9. *Does RM treat all dollar gains of equal value?*

The examples we've used so far do treat all dollar-denominated gains as of equal value. But that's a matter of convenience, not principle.

Consider two job-training programs funded by a poverty-fighting philanthropy. Program 1 trains unemployed workers as carpenters, raising average annual incomes to $15,000 from $10,000. Program 2 trains a different category of unemployed workers as day care workers, raising average annual incomes to $6,000 from $1,000. Each program boosts income by an average of $5,000 per participant. For that reason, Robin Hood treats them as equally good poverty fighters.

But a funder might decide, plausibly enough, to rank Program 2 higher because it delivers the same sized income boost to individuals who start out poorer (earning only $1,000 a year compared with $10,000 for Program 1).

Why precisely might a funder decide to weight some dollar gains differently from others? First, there's something deeply intuitive about the notion that giving $5,000 to individuals scraping by on $1,000 a year transforms the quality of their lives by more than the same sized gift handed to individuals earning $20,000 a year. The intuition is formalized in basic economic models, which assume (in economist speak) diminishing marginal utility of income. In English: If an individual receives successive gifts of $100, each gift would add to the recipient's well-being, but the increases in well-being would grow smaller and smaller. However, this basic economic assumption does not apply across individuals. There is no way to demonstrate unambiguously that a $100 gift for an individual who earns $1,000 a year produces a bigger boost to well-being than does the same $100 gift for an individual who starts out earnings $5,000 a year.

Theoretical underpinning or not, the desire of funders to place extra weight on gains for deeply needy individuals runs deep among nonprofits. The important point here is to recognize that any such desire is the funder's right and should be incorporated explicitly—and consistently—into its grant-making algorithms. If the funder's preference is to help the poorest of the poor, then its equations need to reflect that value judgment.

Robin Hood made some efforts years back to weight dollar gains for very low income families more heavily than the same sized dollar gains for not so low income families. Staff did not have much basis for choosing the weights. But, as it turned out, the weighting schemes it used (somewhat arbitrarily) did not much affect the ranking of grants. It turned out that the individuals Robin Hood then served were overwhelmingly very low income and differential weights did not make much of a change. There is no reason to believe that other funders, or Robin Hood at different times, would come to the same conclusion.

# 10

## Six Purposes

The importance of Relentless Monetization (RM) ranges far beyond ranking of grants. Below we discuss five other purposes.

*First, shared vocabulary for internal deliberations*

Subjecting grant making to the rigor of RM changes the nature of grant-making discussions. Rather than loose talk about inspirational executive directors or creative missions, staff relies on a shared vocabulary that centers on outcomes-based evidence. A program officer who proposes making a grant for grantee AAA knows that the conversation starts, though not finishes, with a recitation of its likely quantitative impact on mission-related benefits. Internal politics, favoritism, habit, difficult personalities never disappear altogether, but all matter less for making grants when conversation focuses on outcomes-based evidence.

*Second, communication with grantees*

A school points to its high graduation rate. A health program points to the large number of neighbors who come for cancer screening. But the funder refuses both requests, sharing with the applicants its calculations for how many students would have succeeded without the applicant's school, or how many neighbors would have received cancer screening without the applicant's help. Once the funder has made clear to the applicants its criteria and how they have been applied in the case at hand, conversation between applicant and funder turns productive. Once the funder makes clear to the applicant what the numbers need to look like to make the application attractive, the grantee's better equipped not just to sharpen its request, but to consider ways to alter its mode of operations so as to be more worthy of support.

*Third, transparency*

RM allows funders to make the algorithms it uses to assign mission-relevant value to interventions available for external scrutiny. Outsiders can examine the lender's equations, assumptions, and rationales, criticize the ones with which they disagree and, most important, propose improvements. So can grantees. Because the funder can publish details of its algorithms, the public can gain ready access.

*Fourth, diagnosis*

Diagnosis is one of RM's two most important purposes.

We've likened the use of benefit/cost ratios in grant making to the use of SAT scores in college admissions. The likeness bears repeating. The key point is that benefit/cost ratios provide a diagnostic tool for grantees, potential grantees, and funders. Funders can scrutinize the operations of grantees that receive high scores and ask, first, are the high scores real—are these groups powerfully fighting poverty or are the high scores aberrant? If the high scores are accurate, what do the grantees share in common and how can the success be replicated?

Funders can scrutinize the operations of low-rated grantees and ask the same questions: (1) Are the low scores accurate or has the funder misestimated the impact, perhaps by overlooking an intangible benefit? The funder needs to question whether its metrics calculations are wrong across the board for specific types of grantees. (2) If the funder comes to the conclusion that the grantee's impact is truly low, what could be done to lift it and would the bigger impact be cost-effective in the precise sense that the funder's money would be better spent fixing the low-scoring group rather than used to create mission-related outcomes some other way?

Robin Hood requires its program officers to compare the estimated benefit/cost ratio before the grant was made to the benefit/cost ratio after the grant year is over. Any large discrepancies drive the staff to ask exactly the right questions: Why did performance lag predictions, or why did performance exceed expectations? Robin Hood also requires staff to estimate benefit/cost ratios five or so years down the road, after staff has had time to expand the grant to its ideal level. That's a good way to diagnose the grantee's potential to scale operations at levels that exploit possible economies.

Program staffers no doubt look first to increase (decrease) grants with high (low) benefit/cost ratios. But nonquantified factors can mitigate, or even reverse, such temptations. For example, some of our groups with high benefit/cost ratios are badly poised to expand.

The ratios lead staff to tackle hard questions. When Robin Hood examined low-ranked job training groups, it cringed. Many at the bottom of the rankings had been the organization's darling, prized grantees. Was staff simply wrong? It turns out that many of its lowest ranked grantees placed trainees in jobs that started out at low wages—thus yielding relatively low year-to-year benefit/cost ratios. But some of these jobs provided good chances for career advancement and, therefore, growing wages over time. Said another way, some low-ranked groups were wrongly measured. Our benefit/cost calculations failed to take career advancement into account. Rather than reducing the grant to these groups, we instead fixed our metric—and increased the size of some of these grants.

Using benefit/cost estimates as fodder for analysis produces surprising truths. Robin Hood's staff had predicted that job training grantees would achieve better success if they would provide social services by their own staff rather than outsourcing the social services. Wrong. The expectation ran counter to the clear weight of the data.

The important point is that RM steers staff attention in all the right places. Metrics guide inquiry. When groups rank surprisingly high or low, the staff asks why. What are the lessons? What are the causes? The new metric leads the staff not only to make smarter decisions, but also to ask the right questions.

*Fifth, ranking grants*

Yes, RM calls for combining benefit/cost ratios estimates with other qualitative information to rank grant applications one against another no matter how dissimilar their purpose. The bulk of the previous chapters have been devoted to this purpose. The numbers have triggered close examinations of specific programs and specific types of programs, leading, in Robin Hood's case, to major changes in grant-making decisions.

*Sixth, measuring the performance of the funder (in addition to that of the grant)*

This is no doubt the most elegant of RM's purposes. The oft-repeated quip directed against funders is that they're quick to assess the impact of anyone and everyone except themselves. However, by the logic of RM, the benefit/cost ratio that measures the impact of the grant also measures, by the exact same number, the performance of the funder. The double-duty served by the benefit/cost ratio follows from the fact that the rules of RM as described in this book dictate that the numerator captures benefits as defined by the funder's mission. It is for that straightforward reason that the benefit/cost ratio perfectly captures the funder's performance, or, in other words, the degree to which the funder has accomplished its mission.

# 11

# Prominent Metrics Systems

This chapter draws brief comparisons between several prominent alternative systems of metrics and Relentless Monetization (RM). We do not make fine-grained comparisons. Instead, we rivet on four large-picture questions.

First, do the metrics systems tackle the hard problem of measuring mission-relevant *outcomes*, or, do they, instead, track simpler to measure *input* focused variables such as costs or numbers of participants?

Take the mission-related value of job training programs to a funder whose mission is fighting poverty. To do metrics right, as we've described, the funder needs to measure the impact of training on future earnings by tracking actual future earnings relative to (estimated) counterfactual earnings. Consider a program that funnels lots of individuals into a program that trains people to become electricians. If the funder uses a metric that tracks the number of enrollees, the program looks good. But is the number of *enrollees* really providing useful information regarding the mission-relevant outcomes? Not necessarily. Suppose most of the enrollees fail to complete the training. Impact on poverty: hardly anything. Or take an electrician training program that *graduates* most of its enrollees. Is the number of graduates (or, for that matter, the percentage of enrollees graduating) really measuring the critical variables? If the funder uses a metric that tracks the number of graduates, the program looks good. But the program may contribute little if anything to poverty fighting if its graduates are poorly trained and fail to acquire long-term employment. Translation: tracking easy to measure outcomes often leads to poor decisions. Measures like enrollment and graduation may tell us something about the *intermediate* steps in preparing individuals to succeed, but they do not constitute measures of success in and of themselves. By contrast, we do treat graduation from high school as an outcome because research shows that graduation is directly linked to better-paying jobs. Armed with the wrong metric, the funder allocates resources in ways that limit the mission-relevant benefit.

Second, does the metrics system handle the comparison of apples to oranges—compare the value of one type of benefit versus that of another? As we'll see, even smart, outcomes-focused funders run around the apples/oranges problem by limiting the scope of their grant making to a single type of intervention. A health group might limit its focus to a single disease. An environmental group might limit its focus to a single waterway. The problem with single-focus funders is that they rule out of consideration many interventions that would achieve their mission better than the interventions they do fund.

Third, does the metrics system take careful account of counterfactual evidence and, if so, how?

Fourth, does the metrics system enable funders to allocate funds coherently and effectively?

Here we review several alternatives to Robin Hood's version of small-bore benefit/cost analysis. In order, we examine:

- Cost-effectiveness analysis
- BACO (best available charitable option) ratio, as developed by the Acumen Fund
- Social rate of return on investment (SROI), as developed by the Roberts Enterprise Development Fund (REDF) and the New Economics Foundation
- Cost-per-impact, as developed by the Center for High Impact Philanthropy
- Expected return, as developed by the Hewlett Foundation
- Charity Navigator

These systems were chosen because they figure prominently in important philanthropic arenas.[1]

## Cost-Effectiveness Analysis

Cost-effectiveness, as discussed in chapter 9, compares the cost per success among two or more grants under the assumption that the grants generate one identical benefit. As such, cost-effectiveness fails the apples/oranges test: It cannot rank the value of a grant that grows apples relative to the value of one that grows oranges. In the world of cost-effectiveness, farmers grow only apples. No oranges allowed. With only one benefit under review, the funder faces no need to compare the value of one benefit versus another or to aggregate across different types of benefits.

Take two nonprofits. They share the same mission. They each train unemployed workers to become entry level electricians. They draw trainees from a single pool of applicants. Compare the effectiveness of the two nonprofits. Define "success" as a trainee that graduates the training program with the necessary skills. A cost-effectiveness metric would compare the cost per graduate for one nonprofit versus that for the other. Note that the denominator of this metric—the number of trainees who graduate the training program with the appropriate skills—can be measured in physical units. No need to use dollars. No need, therefore, to monetize outcomes (relentlessly or otherwise).

Suppose, for example, that Nonprofit 1 spends $5,000 to train each electrician, but Nonprofit 2 spends only $4,000 per success. Assume that the two nonprofits share a single funder. If that funder reduces its grant to Nonprofit 1 by $100,000, then it will cut the number of trained electricians by 20 ($100,000/$5,000). And if that funder hands the $100,000 over to Nonprofit 2, then the number of trained electricians will rise by 25 ($100,000/$4,000). Without spending an extra dime, the lender has increased the number of trained electricians by five.

The virtue of a cost-effectiveness metric is its simplicity and ease of use. Cost-effectiveness proves valuable when comparing the performance of nonprofits that generate identical outcomes. In the preceding example, a funder that finds itself funding the high cost nonprofit will surely want to re-examine its decision.

But ponder how the simplicity of cost-effectiveness metrics shatters when circumstances change, however slightly. What if Nonprofit 1 trains carpenters as well as electricians? Counting electricians no longer suffices as a measure of success. A funder would need to calculate the aggregate value of training not just electricians but carpenters as well. To add the value of training electricians to that of training carpenters, the funder would need to adopt a unit of measurement that allows for the comparison of electricians and carpenters. That unit of measurement is almost always the dollar and the process of assigning dollar values to electricians and carpenters is what we called "monetization."

Let's tweak circumstances in another way. Nonprofit 1 spends 25 percent more to train electricians than does Nonprofit 2 because, at least in part, Nonprofit 1 turns out better trained electricians. If so, then the assumption behind the previous analysis—that the two grantees generate one, identical benefit—is violated. An electrician newly trained by Nonprofit 1 will earn more on average than will a newly trained electrician by Nonprofit 2. The outcomes from the two programs are not identical. Simple head counts from each program—and cost-effectiveness measures based on those head counts—will not capture important differences between the two programs.

Here's another tweak. What if the folks who train to become electricians are better off economically than are those who train to become carpenters? Expressed equivalently, what if the counterfactual earnings of the would-be electricians exceed the counterfactual earnings of the would-be carpenters? In this case, training an electrician might raise the individual's future earnings by less than training a carpenter would. If so, simple head counts—and cost-effectiveness calculations based on those head counts—would fail to capture important differences between the two programs.

The downside of cost-effectiveness measures is that they rule out by assumption the complexity that governs the world in which we live. How does a funder use cost-effectiveness measures when deciding between funding a program that trains electricians drawn from an applicant pool that includes only ex-offenders and one that trains electricians drawn from an applicant pool that includes only students enrolled in community colleges? The answer is that it doesn't. The funder needs to answer the question: Which nonprofit generates the most impact per dollar? In the real world, that requires comparing nonidentical benefits. That's a question that RM answers but cost-effectiveness metrics do not.

## Acumen Fund's Best Available Charitable Option Measure

The Acumen Fund's version of smart metrics, BACO (best available charitable option), does indeed embrace the fundamental principle of benefit/cost analysis. Projects under review are compared with alternative uses of philanthropic dollars. But, and this is an important but, comparisons are limited only to projects of similar type. For example, if Acumen were considering funding a project to install energy efficient, nonpolluting cook stoves in sub-Saharan homes, it would compare the impact of one such project to another (differing, perhaps, in location). Or if Acumen were considering a project to provide miracle seeds to poor Third World farmers, it would find another seed-distribution project for purposes of comparison.

The restricted nature of BACO comparisons serves an attractive purpose: simplification. BACO compares grants of similar type. Therefore, benefits of the project under review and the project to which it is compared can be measured in the same natural units (cook stoves installed; number of farmers receiving miracle seeds). That reduces Acumen's task to that of calculating cost effectiveness (cost per output). With BACO, there is no need for a methodology that can aggregate across different types of outcomes. And BACO can avoid placing explicit dollar value on hard to measure benefits.

The downside is that BACO suffers from some of the limitations of cost-effectiveness metrics. BACO does not direct funding decisions across different kinds of projects, for example, installing cook stoves versus distributing miracle seeds. BACO's simplicity comes at a steep price. It does not truly identify the best available charitable option. At best, it identifies the best project of the *exact same type*. Between those two claims lies a chasm of difference.

## Social Rate of Return on Investment

The measure SROI shares some key principles of the benefit/cost analysis that undergirds RM. And, like RM, SROI explicitly aggregates separately estimated partial impacts to derive an estimate of overall impact, but there's an all-important difference between SROI and RM. That difference is the point of view from which all calculations are made. SROI makes calculations from the perspective of an enterprise. Specifically, the SROI formula assigns a social value to enterprises, calculated as the sum of the economic value of the enterprise's commercial operations plus a quantified value of social externalities that the enterprise generates. Relentless Monetization, by contrast, answers a chiseled question: What decision should the funder make to best support its mission?

Take the example of a commercial enterprise that hires disabled individuals to do outdoor maintenance. The numerator of the SROI for the enterprise consists of the sum of (1) the present discounted value of the outdoor maintenance business; and (2) the estimated net value of the social savings from hiring previously unemployed, disabled individuals (calculated as the net reduction in government expenditures and increase in tax revenues). The SROI ratio is computed by dividing the numerator of the enterprise by the total investment (from all sources) it requires, thereby completing the analog to a corporate rate of return.

Consider evaluation of a commercial enterprise using SROI. It counts as benefits both the created present value of the commercial enterprise and reductions in public support payments for the workers who will be employed. But suppose the commercial enterprise could be organized in a different way so it could get its work done with fewer employees. The present value of the business would rise. But government support payments for unemployed workers would not fall (or at least would not fall by nearly as much). The question becomes, how should the two impacts be weighted relative to one another? If, for example, if the SROI computation finds that the net effect of the two factors is near zero, should the funder be indifferent as to how the enterprise is organized? If the two impacts are not equally important, what is the correct tradeoff between them? The SROI methodology does not appear to provide much guidance.

RM, by contrast, estimates value from the point of view of a decision maker with a specific mission. To a practitioner of RM, the computation of SROI can appear as a hodgepodge, taking no consistent account of the benefits and costs from the point of view of any one decision maker or from the point of view of any other specific objective.

Another difference between RM and SROI—more in implementation than in theory—is that SROI analyses do not take consistent account of counterfactual values. Finally, as a practical matter, the number of completed analyses appears modest, suggesting that the process is cumbersome and perhaps expensive to resource constrained funders.

### Cost-per-Impact

The Center for High Impact Philanthropy developed cost-per-impact as a measure of philanthropic effectiveness. In theory, the measure can be viewed as the inverse of benefit/cost analysis, which could just as easily be called impact-per-cost. But in practice, cost-per-impact operates more like a cost-effectiveness standard.

The center's metric has been used to estimate the cost of achieving a single, primary benefit. For example, a study of a malaria intervention measured impact by estimating the number of children under the age of five who lived because of the intervention. A literacy training project in the United States was measured by the boost to the number of students meeting literacy standards. And so on.

The metric takes all due account of counterfactuals. But, as we've seen with cost-effectiveness and several other metrics, the cost-per-impact metric has not been developed in a way that allows for comparison of interventions that generate *different* types of benefits. The center's studies do not aggregate across separate categories of benefits.

### Expected Return

The William and Flora Hewlett Foundation's "expected-return" criterion for making grants fits comfortably the principles underlying RM.[2] The foundation estimates the impact of a proposed grant by multiplying the monetized benefit of a potential grant if it proves successful—the benefit that would result "in a perfect world"—by the probability of success. The calculation yields the numerator of the project's expected benefit/cost ratio. By way of contrast, RM involves no construction of "a perfect world." Nor does RM create a simplified divide between success and failure. That said, the Hewlett Foundation's basic calculation roughly follows the outlines of Robin Hood's risk-neutral approach to RM as discussed in chapter 9.

Expected Return and RM have been implemented for different purposes. Here's one such difference. Hewlett applies its method to big projects, to what it calls "large scale policy change investments." Examples include projects to protect waterways; evaluate procedures by which to hold governments with histories of corruption accountable for public expenditures; and regulate development of energy sources. Thus, the size and purpose of the projects to which Expected Return has been applied differ greatly from the size and purpose of the projects to which RM has been applied. The scale and purpose of projects do not affect the theory behind the analysis, but they surely affect what types of benefits are worth the time and effort to monetize. To take an admittedly extreme example, the analysis of the impact of a dam on countrywide economic growth might well dismiss the need to monetize the value of free showers for construction workers. But an analysis of services that an emergency food center provides homeless adults might feel compelled to figure out the importance of showers.

### Charity Navigator

Imagine that you want to donate to one or more nonprofits but you lack the time or expertise to choose wisely. Which of the thousands of nonprofits are scams? Which, perhaps despite the best of intentions, engage in wasteful, if not inept, activities? Your inability to distinguish the good guys from the bad guys can steer you away from unknown, scrappy start-ups in favor of well-known, seemingly safe nonprofits. Worse, the danger of giving to the wrong programs might discourage you from donating at all.

Enter Charity Navigator (CN), itself a nonprofit that rates over 5,000 other nonprofits on a large number of variables. Our point? CN's numbers can be modestly useful, but only if the reader fully understands their limitations. Taken at face value, the numbers can mislead.[3]

Here is a quote directly from the CN Web site.

> Accountability is an obligation or willingness by a charity to explain its actions to its stakeholders. For now, Charity Navigator is specifically evaluating the fiduciary actions of charities. In the future, we intend to evaluate other aspects of accountability such as results reporting and other indicators of the way organizations use the resources they raise to accomplish their mission.

In short, CN focuses on costs, on potential waste. That's useful. But here's another instance of a nonprofit report card that rules out the hard task of measuring benefits. As we've painstakingly argued, the fixation on costs to the exclusion of benefits leads to wrongheaded conclusions. Low costs are not a virtue in and of themselves. Nonprofits can rack up low costs because they provide shoddy services or because they serve individuals who don't need much help. The right—indeed, only—way to evaluate a nonprofit's operation is to balance the benefits it generates against the costs it incurs.

That said, costs do matter, especially if they reflect waste. On some cost-based matters, CN offers highly valuable information. For example, it tracks transparency and accountability to ferret out scams. CN defines transparency as "an obligation or willingness by a charity to publish and make available critical data about the organization," and defines accountability as "an obligation or willingness by a charity to explain its actions to its stakeholders." For each nonprofit that it reviews, the Web site provides answers to important questions: who sits on the nonprofit's board; and whether the nonprofit makes public regularly scheduled audits by independent auditors.

CN also reports seven measures of "financial health." Four of these measures track "financial efficiency performance." What fraction of a nonprofit's total budget covers the cost of its programs (the reason that the nonprofit exists)? What fraction of total expenses covers administrative costs and fundraising costs? How much of each dollar raised from donors is spent on the fundraising activities themselves? The remaining three waste-related measures track financial capacity, "how well it (the nonprofit under review) has sustained its programs and services over time, and whether it can continue to do so." The Web site reports the rates at which the non-profit's outlays on programs and fundraising totals have been growing—the faster, the better, CN implies. Finally, CN examines the nonprofit's working capital ratio, defined as the value of unrestricted assets as a percent of the nonprofit's budget. CN uses the ratio to indicate how well the nonprofit can weather unexpected financial shortfalls.

We question the usefulness of these measures of financial capacity. Why, as CN suggests, is a nonprofit that has successfully achieved its mission for many years at the same scale of operation any less likely to survive than is a nonprofit that has been recently growing at pell-mell speed? We note that CN's measure of working capital provides a financial snapshot of the nonprofit's operation at no more than a single moment in time and the ratio excludes key considerations of financial sustainability, such as the strength of the nonprofit's ties to its donors.

But the pros and cons of CN's "financial efficiency performance metrics" aren't the issue at this juncture of the book. Instead, we draw the reader's attention to the remarks we made at the beginning of the discussion of CN: by excluding measures of benefits, the Web site cannot provide a systematic guide to success. The right way to evaluate performance is to answer how much value, appropriately defined, does a nonprofit generate per dollar of cost? This is the benefit/cost test that lies at the core of RM. Dealing with costs is (relatively) easy. Dealing with benefits, as we've seen throughout this book, is far harder. By focusing solely on costs, donors who visit CN's Web site risk shutting their wallets to nonprofits that incur high costs because they provide high value benefits.

CN invites the visitors to its Web site to think "Waste, Fraud, and Abuse." Fraud and abuse are real problems, and CN can help donors avoid them. But what is likely to be the bigger problem, waste or ineptness? Asked another way, which of the following two nonprofits would you rather fund? Nonprofit 1 is wasteful but smart. It pays excessively high salaries to staff, wasting 10 percent of its budget. But it achieves a 10:1 benefit/cost ratio on the other 90 percent of its budget. Here, donors generate $9 dollars of mission-related benefits for every dollar they donate. Compare that result to donations to Nonprofit 2. It wastes nothing but achieves only a 1:1 benefit/

cost ratio on its program budget. In this case, donors generate only $1 of good for every dollar they donate. What does CN's Web site have to say about the choice? Its metrics tell readers that Nonprofit 2 wastes no money. That's a fact worth celebrating. But another important fact about Nonprofit 2 is that it does very little good with the dollars it spends, surely a fact worth criticizing. CN tells the former story but not the latter.

Why hasn't CN tackled the challenge of tracking benefits? As we've shown throughout this book, tracking benefits that come in different shapes and sizes is hard, requiring machinery that mirrors that of RM. Given the kind of performance data most nonprofits collect and make public, CN simply has no basis for rating nonprofits on effectiveness. By using a rating system that penalizes nonprofits that spend a higher portion of their total expenses on administrative overhead, CN may actually be praising the least effective agencies. Good metrics don't come easily. The complexity of RM exists for good reason.

Imagine a different Web-based scorecard. This imaginary Web site rates nonprofits according to the metrics dictated by smart philanthropy. Here, nonprofits not only report how much they spend, but also how much benefit they achieve (as dictated by their missions). Then we would have the kind of "transparency and accountability" that matter, the kind that allow visitors to the Web site to distinguish smart from not-so-smart non-profits. We'd have the information to address not just fraud, not just abuse, but also waste in the economist's sense of that term. We'd have the infor-mation to determine which nonprofits spend money in the most powerful ways possible.

The purpose of these brief comparisons among systems of metrics (including a scorecard), as we stated at the outset, is not to provide de-tailed comparisons. Our purpose is simpler. Metrics systems, even those that focus on measured outcomes, differ in fundamental ways. The reader needs to keep those differences in mind. We reinforce four pressing questions.

1. Does the metrics system focus attention on outcomes as defined by the nonprofit's mission or instead on easier-to-measure but poten-tially misleading variables such as inputs or costs per enrollee or headcounts?

2. Does the metrics system take explicit account of different types of benefits? Specifically, does the system permit comparisons of differ-ent kinds of programs with different kinds of benefits?

3. Does the metrics system pay scrupulously careful attention to counterfactuals?

4. Does the metrics systems focus funder attention on a coherent set of variables?

A number of metrics systems are under development, especially among philanthropies that operate in underdeveloped countries. One prediction seems safe. The capacity of charities to marshal data on behalf of program analysis will soar. Whether the emerging capacity will be used correctly is harder to predict.

# 12

# Reflections on Risk

In our discussion of Relentless Monetization (RM), we have so far taken no explicit account of risk, the fact that philanthropists cannot know for sure the impact of their interventions. This chapter makes amends with the following broad points.

- Funders, to best fulfill their missions, need to take account of the risks that their decisions impose on the intended beneficiaries. We label this obligation the "good steward" responsibility.
- Funders when addressing issues of risk might well resort to simple rules of thumb. We offer our own to guide decisions about small, modestly risky grants.
- For large grants that impose sizeable risks for the funder's intended beneficiaries, we set out a more elaborate conceptual framework; in effect, a generalization of the benefit/cost apparatus presented in chapter 8.
- The notion of "real options valuation," a fundamental feature of the literature on managing financial risk, can be usefully applied to philanthropic decisions.
- So too, the notion of game changers—investments that substantially alter the economic landscape of which they are a part—can be usefully applied to philanthropic decisions.

## Risk: Good and Bad

Risk is two sided. On one side, philanthropists crave high payoffs (upside potential) from hitherto untested initiatives—a craving that's been encouraged by the rise in the number of risk-seeking "venture philanthropists." But on the other side, philanthropists shun failures. They threaten the well-being of target populations and potentially repel potential donors.

So far in our discussion of RM, we've taken the simplest possible approach to risk. Specifically, we've assumed that funders make risk-neutral choices, guided by expected benefit,[1] that neither crave risk (in pursuit of higher return) nor shun it (in pursuit of certainty). This is what Robin Hood has done until now. But risk-neutrality is in no sense a requirement of RM, let alone any other form of rational decision making. Deliberating how best to deal with risk is on Robin Hood's agenda and needs to be on that of any thoughtful funder.

Our premise is that funders *should* care about risk. How they handle it is important for the targeted beneficiaries.

If funders back risky initiatives that fail, target individuals lose out. Sometimes they lose because funders who back risky projects do not as a consequence back less risky projects that would have generated important benefits for the intended beneficiaries. What is lost is the foregone opportunity. Some projects impose direct risks. For example, an initiative to promote small-scale entrepreneurship might require targeted participants to take out loans that they won't be able to repay if the start-up businesses collapse. Similarly, a project to restore an endangered species might wind up destroying the very habitat it was aiming to preserve.

But failing to take risks can also harm the target population. If, to reduce the chances of failure, funders back only interventions that offer smaller but more certain returns, then they may well deny the target population any real shot at big gains. Take the example of a funder considering two possible projects. Project 1 would fund a longshot effort to find a miracle cure for obesity, a plague in low income urban communities. This is a classic example of a project that offers low odds of success but gigantic gains if successful. Project 2 would train unemployed parents to fill back office, low paid jobs in the private sector. This is a classic example of a project that offers high odds of success, but only modest gains if successful. Which is the better choice? There is no obvious answer.

If funders are going to be able attract funding and allocate it wisely, they need to take proper account of risk when deciding what grants to make and when talking to potential donors. This chapter introduces the concept of risk as it applies to philanthropic endeavors and discusses ways funders can deal with risk within the context of RM.

## Attitudes Toward Risk

Let's start with nomenclature.

First, we use the terms "funders" and "donors" interchangeably, and we refer to mission-relevant beneficiaries of the programs funded by donors as the "target population" or "target individuals."

Second, we describe a program as involving risk if the outcome of the program can't be predicted confidently. We use the expression "greater risk" to mean that the range of possible future outcomes, good or bad, has widened,[2] and the expression "downside risk" to mean the prospect of undesirable outcomes.

Third, we borrow social science terminology that characterizes attitudes toward risk by grouping individuals into three camps—risk-neutral, risk-averse, and risk-preferring.

Consider an individual deciding whether to invest $1,000 in a venture that has two outcomes: (1) a 50 percent chance of failing completely, yielding a loss of the entire $1,000; or (2) a 50 percent chance of yielding gross benefits of $2,000 for a net gain of $1,000 ($2,000 gross benefits minus the original $1,000 investment). The expected value of making the $1,000 investment is zero [expected value = (0.5 × –$1,000) + (0.5 × $1,000) = $0].[3] A risk-neutral person takes into account nothing other than expected value. Because expected value is zero in this example, risk-neutral individuals would be indifferent between making and not making this investment. Individuals who are risk-preferring would make the investment despite its zero expected net benefit because they crave the upside potential (the prospect of winning $1,000). Risk-averse individuals would not choose the investment because they would be more fearful of the downside potential (losing $1,000) than attracted by the upside potential.

Before we discuss *why* different people might react differently to the same investment opportunity, let's change the example slightly to clarify what it means to be risk-preferring and risk-averse.

Suppose that the initial investment necessary to launch the venture was only $800 rather than $1,000. The project costs the investor $800 if it fails and generates $1,200 ($2,000 – $800) of profit if it succeeds. The expected outcome of this project equals $200 [(0.5 × -$800) + (0.5 × $1,200)], which is a positive number. What decision would individuals make now? Risk-preferring individuals would surely invest. By contrast to the first example, risk-neutral individuals, by paying attention only to expected value, would prefer to invest than not invest. Risk-averse individuals might or might not.

Why might the same project appeal to one person and not another? Why might a person pass up an investment with a positive expected dollar payoff? The answer to both questions lies in the fact that when people consider making risky investments, they don't limit their attention to the impact of the investment on their wealth. They focus on something broader—well-being (what economists call utility). The distinction is all-important because, in general, wealth and well-being do not move in direct proportion to one another. Think of increasing an individual's wealth in increments of $500. For most people, each new increment adds to the individual's well-being. But the addition to well-being grows smaller and smaller with each increment. The intuition is straightforward. Adding $500 to the income of a family whose income is only $2,000 to begin with is a big, big deal. But adding $500 to the income of a family that starts out at $100,000 is a much smaller deal.

By implication individuals do not, in general, treat monetary gains and losses symmetrically. They often place more value on avoiding losses than they do on reaping equal-sized gains. Winning a $10,000 lottery ticket provides a welcomed windfall. But losing $10,000 can wreck the family's financial foundation. The upside value of winning $10,000 falls short of the downside loss from losing $10,000. The point of these preliminary remarks is that the choice individuals make among risky options is not a simple matter of arithmetic. The arithmetic of gains and losses differs across individuals because we all place different weights on monetary gains and losses. Said another way, individuals translate upside and downside outcomes according to their idiosyncratic measures of well-being.

Consider our example in the previous paragraph. If you are a wealthy person and all that is at stake is $800 on the downside and $1,200 on the upside, the well-being you would sacrifice for each of the dollars you might lose on the downside is not going to differ much or at all from the well-being you would get from each dollar you might gain on the upside; therefore, positive expected dollar gain translates to positive expected change in well-being. But if you are poor—if all you have is $800—and then you lose, you become destitute. The fewer dollars you have, the more painful it is to lose one of them. As a poor person, given the size of the potential loss and gain, the well-being you would lose on the downside would very likely be far greater than the well-being you would gain on the upside. From the perspective of the expected change in your *well-being*, given the 50–50 chance of each outcome, making this investment looms as a bad choice.

## The "Good Steward" Perspective

We make two points here. First, funders, to fulfill their missions, in most situations need to adopt the risk profile of their target populations. Second, in lieu of the difficulty, and perhaps impossibility, of making detailed calculations, we urge funders to adopt a rule of thumb to guide how much risk its grant making should impose on targeted individuals. Toward that end, we recommend a safe harbor, explained in the next several paragraphs.

As our stylized examples show, the expected impact of a risky investment on personal well-being depends on the individual's tolerance for risk. But whose tolerance should guide a *funder's* decisions?[4] Should it be that of the donors, who provide the resources? Donors, if wealthy, are likely to tolerate risk and, as we'll discuss, may well have a positive attitude toward risk. Or should the funder make decisions according to the risk preferences of its target population?

We argue, as we've done consistently throughout this book, that a funder needs to make decisions that best fulfill its mission. In general, that imperative will be met best by taking account of the risk preferences of its target population. That said, we pronounce no ironclad rule. For example, suppose that by exercising a higher toleration for risk than does the target population, a funder attracts increased donations from donors. If so, then the funder might better serve its intended beneficiaries by taking on more risk than it would by taking on less risk. But we can conjecture that such circumstances are rare. To assume a risk profile radically different from one's target population risks serving the preferences of the funder at the expense of its mission. Once a funder has identified its target population, whether that population consists of people or penguins or protozoa or paintings, it should serve as the steward of that population's interests.[5] If the target population consists of individuals for whom a loss of philanthropy-provided benefits might be extremely costly, the funder should allocate its resources in ways that properly take into account the consequences for those individuals, including the potential sacrifice of well-being they will suffer if risky philanthropic ventures fail to pan out. We call this the "good steward responsibility."

It might appear at first glance that adhering to our good-steward responsibility would necessarily require funders whose mission is to serve vulnerable populations to eliminate their programmatic risk taking or, at least to reduce it significantly. Not necessarily. A good steward funder, acting in the best interests of its target population, should not avert risk excessively or be paralyzed by the presence of risk. The dispositive choices are between more risk versus less risk, rather than some risk versus no risk. It makes no philanthropic sense to sacrifice important mission-relevant benefits just to reduce by a minor amount any single risk of the many faced by the target population.

Per capita impact is a key consideration we deem essential to philanthropic decisions. If the impact of a funder's programs on the individuals in its target population is small per capita, then allocating funds to a risky initiative will not put the target population much at risk if the project fails.

We acknowledge that "small per capita" is a vague phrase, but we've found no good alternative. We commend the following rule of thumb, the 3 percent rule.

*A funder fulfills its good steward obligation to protect its target population from excessive risk if, were all its projects to fail, the total loss of well-being for the target population would amount to less than 3 percent of its pre-intervention income.*[6]

If its projects obey the 3 percent rule of thumb, the funder can proceed and yet protect its target population from excessive risk. No more is required. We argue that the 3 percent safe harbor provides a reasonable guide in circumstances in which more detailed calculations are infeasible.

Our argument is not that our 3 percent rule of thumb should apply to all funders under any and all circumstances. It enjoys no such scientific foundation. Rather, we argue that funders need some easy-to-apply guideline that makes plausible sense in the context of their missions. We offer ours for discussion within the philanthropic community in the hope that others will use it to help refine their own. That said, our 3 percent rule of thumb is not completely arbitrary. We arrived at it on the basis of two approaches, one relying more on our "feel" of the circumstances of at least one target population, the other relying more on a formal analytical exercise. We discuss these in turn.

Consider a person with an annual income that averages about $10,000. Three percent of that income is $300, which we recognize is not a trivial sum on so low a base. However, when considered in the context of the far larger financial risks faced by low income individuals—for example, those associated with illness or job loss—the amount at risk does not loom large. Further, $300 comes to a daily sacrifice of a bit under $1, which is well below the cost of any number of relatively common small expenditures. We felt that if this is the sacrifice associated with a downside outcome of a promising risky initiative, it is a manageable one.

The second approach we employed to arrive at our 3 percent rule was more formal. Essentially, we performed many numerical simulation experiments to investigate the impact of philanthropic risk taking on the expected well-being of a typical low income target individual. Each simulation incorporated different assumptions regarding five variables: (1) the dollar income of a target individual; (2) the benefit/cost ratio achieved by a safe intervention; (3) the share of funding diverted from safe to a risky intervention; (4) the expected benefit/cost and riskiness of the risky intervention; and (5) the level of the target individual's aversion to risk,[7] the latter drawn from the academic literature[8] on risk aversion.

The results of these simulations indicated that if we made reasonable assumptions regarding all the key variables, and if the downside risk was limited to 3 percent of pre-intervention income, then the change in expected well-being produced by pursuing a risky intervention was slight, sometimes positive and sometimes negative. These results gave us some confidence that our intuitively derived benchmark is not far off the mark.

Consider what our 3 percent rule of thumb implies for funders' allocation of resources to risky initiatives. Take a funder whose programs amount to about 15 percent of the collective incomes of the target population. Assume the funder's projects could add to the income of the target population, but not reduce them. If the funder would place 20 percent of its grants in risky initiatives and those initiatives failed completely, then the income of targeted individuals would fall by 3 percent—our safe harbor—below what income would be had the funder chosen safe projects [20 percent × 15 percent = 3 percent]. But if the funder's programs bulked smaller, say amounting to only 10 percent of the target population's collective income, then the funder could put a larger amount of its money, 30 percent, at risk and still pass the 3 percent safe harbor test. And if the worst outcome is positive instead of zero, then the proportion that the funder could place in risky projects could rise and yet satisfy the 3 percent rule. Finally, if the worst outcome is negative—if the risky project fails and targeted individuals are left worse off than before the project started—then the maximum the funder could allocate to the risky project and still satisfy the safe harbor test would fall. And so on.

Can a rule of thumb like ours allow a good steward funder to put aside worries about the riskiness of its initiatives? We think yes more often than one might think, even for funders with sizeable grant making budgets. It should be reassuring that a funder with $10 million to spend per year will be spending just $100 per capita if it spreads its funding evenly over a 100,000 target population. And even with high benefit/cost ratios, if the programs generate benefits over extended periods of time, then the *annual* per capita downside risk of risky projects will most likely be small, even for low income target populations. Indeed, in situations like this, a funder almost certainly could make decisions solely based on expected benefits (by contrast to expected utility) without regret.[9]

What all this means is that there is a surefire way by which funders can protect targeted individuals from excessive risk: simply limit the amount or proportion of resources going to high risk initiatives. And this limit works even for funders whose initiatives *do* have a significant impact on their target populations.

That said, not every funder will be in a position either to ignore its target population's risk exposure or adopt a simple rule of thumb that allows it to satisfy its good steward obligation. Sometimes a funder's impact on the target population, or on particular groups within that population, is deep. Each funder needs to look at its mission, scale of operations and expenditures, and size and situation of its target population to assess its own position in this regard.[10]

## Beyond Rules of Thumb: Explicit Accounting for Risk

How should a funder respond when treating risk naively clashes with its good steward obligation? A glib response for anyone familiar with financial markets might be to recommend that the funder should manage risk through diversification. Diversification would call for funding many different projects so that no one threatens the target population. But few philanthropies fund enough projects for diversification to be a realistic option. Nor *should* most philanthropists resort to funding lots of projects. As we discuss in the section of this chapter that addresses real options valuation, funding small projects in the service of diversification can both weaken impact and greatly complicate efforts to accurately measure it. This is not the right strategy.

Funders do have some other ways to approach the issue of risk. One is to explicitly evaluate initiatives on the basis of their expected contribution to target population *well-being* rather than their expected monetized benefit. This amounts to a generalization of the benefit/cost apparatus from chapter 8—a generalization that a funder can invoke if risk neutrality distorts grant making. A second approach is to structure projects so they impose less risk. We consider both approaches in turn.

## Maximizing Expected Well-being

In theory, the right way to handle choice in the presence of risk is to alter the benefit/cost apparatus that we developed in chapter 8 and beyond. From the preceding discussion, we know that income and well-being do not move in perfect tandem. Successive equal additions in income, for most people, generate smaller and smaller additions to well-being. Making good choices when risk is significant and unavoidable requires that the funder, rather than maximize the expected value of mission-relevant dollar benefits,[11] instead maximize the expected well-being of its target population, taking the impact of risk on well-being explicitly into account.

Rather than starting with the general principles behind allocating resources to maximize target individuals' expected well-being and then applying them to an example, we'll start out with a concrete example and extract the general principles.

Assume that a funder has a total annual budget of $5 million and that it has winnowed its spending options to three potential program grants. Each serves the members of its target population and each, individually, would exhaust the $5 million budget. The options are: (1) a "safe" financial literacy program; (2) a "modestly risky" job training program; and (3) a "high risk" nutrition education program.

Some more assumptions follow:

- The funder has a target population of 10,000 on which to spend its $5 million.
- Each member of the target population earns $10,000 per year.
- The funder spends $500 on each member of the target population.
- *All* programmatic benefits accrue *within the year* in which the money is spent.
- The safe financial literacy program achieves a sure benefit/cost ratio of 12.

- The modestly risky job training program has a 50 percent chance of achieving a benefit/cost ratio of 6 and a 50 percent chance of achieving a benefit/cost ratio of 21.
- The high risk nutrition education program has a 10 percent probability of a benefit/cost ratio of 2, a 40 percent probability of 6, a 40 percent probability of 21, and a 10 percent probability of 30.

The first thing to notice is that the right choice is no longer obvious. Given the $500 spending per target individual and the range of the benefit/cost ratios, the amounts at stake are large enough per capita that the well-being generated by the different outcomes cannot be assumed to rise and fall in direct proportion to the dollar value of the outcomes.

Second, in terms of *dollar benefits*, no program clearly dominates any other in the sense of offering a higher expected benefit/cost ratio without absorbing more risk. The financial literacy program offers a sure benefit/cost ratio of 12. The job training program offers a higher expected benefit/cost ratio of 13.5, but has a 50 percent chance of yielding a benefit/cost ratio of just 6. What about the riskier still nutrition education program? It has the highest expected benefit/cost ratio, 14, but it carries the worst downside risk.[12] What's best depends on the dollar gains, the probabilities, and the manner in which the target individuals translate gains in dollars into gains in well-being.

Computing the expected well-being of a philanthropic intervention involves a relatively straightforward extension of the computations used in earlier chapters to compute the expected benefit of interventions—the numerator of the intervention's benefit/cost ratio. Indeed, the computation is the same except that the funder measures outcomes in terms of well-being rather than income (and income equivalents, like the monetized value of health status). To do that, the funder needs to assign to each possible outcome a value of well-being in place of expected dollar benefits. The funder can use the probabilities of different outcomes from the calculation of the benefit/cost ratio in combination with the levels of well-being associated with each possible outcome to derive the expected benefit of an intervention on the target population. The program offering the highest expected well-being is the best of the three. The most challenging part of the exercise is to think about its target population and its needs, and to arrive at a best estimate of the well-being per dollar at various income levels. For those interested in the details, we provide a step-by-step example of this process in appendix C.

Let's take stock. If philanthropic interventions impose substantial risk on target populations, then funders need to take that important fact into account. Specifically, funders need to take the target population's attitudes toward risk into account. Translation: The funder moves from choosing interventions that maximize expected benefits per dollar spent—the numerator of the benefit/cost ratios from chapter 8—to interventions that maximize expected well-being per dollar spent. Those two computations differ because income and well-being do not move in lockstep.

There is a lot of estimating and guesstimating in this process, but it has several important benefits. First, it provides the basis for consistent decisions. Second, the process allows for consistent incorporation of new information about the target population, probabilities of achieving specific outcomes, and availability of new interventions. Third, and perhaps even more important, if the rankings of the programs based on the estimates of the population's utility per dollar and the other information seem somehow to clash with the choice that "feels right," it provides a signal to the funder to re-examine the assumptions, estimates, and guesstimates on which it has been relying in allocating its funding. Sometimes that process will lead a funder to revise those assumptions, estimates, and guesstimates. Other times it will lead the funder to conclude that the choice that felt right was not, in fact, right. As we have systematically argued, relentless quantification makes possible testing and retesting choices in light of evidence.

### Lessons from Real Options Valuation

Beyond taking proper account of the risks that attach to their funding decisions, funders can also manage risk smartly. One way to do that is to borrow a technique, real options valuation (ROV), that financial institutions use to manage risk.[13]

Recall the example, outlined in the preceding section, of the funder facing the choice of a safe financial literacy program, a modestly risky job training program or a high risk nutrition education program. One might argue that the job training program offered the highest expected well-being, even though nutrition education offered the highest expected (monetized) benefit because the threat of the downside loss of the latter outweighed the prospect of its upside potential (even though the average gain was a positive number). But what if there was a way you could capture the upside gain *without* incurring the threat of a more significant downside loss? And what if you could restructure the intervention so the upside potential was even larger, but the downside potential remained the same? Restructuring interventions to better manage risks is what ROV allows funders to do.

At the heart of ROV lies the notion of structuring investments in ways that take advantage of opportunities to respond to new information.[14] Developed to manage risk of financial investments, ROV has proved useful in valuing nonfinancial investments, such as the purchase of oilfield leases and mineral rights. In the analysis that follows, we take matters one step further, applying the logic of ROV to risky philanthropic choices.

As the term "options" suggests, ROV applies to situations in which making an initial investment gives the investors the ability to decide whether to increase or decrease their commitments at subsequent junctures. Future decisions will be based on unfolding events. It is the dynamic nature of decision making that distinguishes ROV from standard calculations of expected value. The latter is static calculation, made at the time of an initial investment. The former builds in future decision points as a risk management device.

Consider a funder that is deciding whether to fund a daring jobs training program. If the funder were to focus on the expected benefit of the investment during the demonstration phase alone, it would reject the intervention in many instances. First, the probability of success of truly innovative ideas is small. The upfront costs of a new program can loom large. And by limiting the analysis to the demonstration phase, the investor would be overlooking the benefits from expanding the project if it indeed proves successful during the demonstration phase. The calculation might not look all that much better if the funder's analysis extended past the demonstration phase to a full rollout. The probability of success for untested ideas would remain low and the costs of a full rollout would loom large.

Standard approaches to benefit/cost analysis make static calculations. They take no account of the ways that the funder could use information collected along the way to change the size of the downside risks and upside potential.

The ROV approach explicitly assumes that investors can actively respond to unfolding events, exploiting the good opportunities that arise and avoiding the paths that lead to bad outcomes.[15] Although the formal theoretical aspects of ROV are anything but obvious, the idea that a funder should actively monitor the progress of its initiatives and respond to circumstances as they unfold seems more than sensible. To the extent that the funder makes adjustments along the way to exploit upside opportunities and diminish downside risks, the prospects for any given risky initiative become better.

Let's use the term "decision juncture" to refer to an opportunity for the funder to change the level or nature of its commitment to a risky initiative. Some risky initiatives naturally allow more decision junctures than others. Projects that call on investors to make an irrevocable commitment up front leave funders with no option to change course in the wake of new information. Said another way, such projects allow for no decision junctures. Other projects, by contrast, allow for modest mid-course corrections and some allow for enormous flexibility. A funder can design an intervention so that as the intervention unfolds and generates data, it has several decision junctures at which it can choose to expand or prune the scale of intervention.

Let's consider what a funder must do to maximize the potential of a risky initiative. First, the funder needs to ensure that there are sufficient decision junctures and the junctures are timely. Next, it must ensure that it will arrive at each decision juncture with the information necessary to make well-informed decisions. In the case of a demonstration project, the funder should design the initiative from its inception with an eye to generating and analyzing data in time to make smart decisions at each decision juncture.

Here we encounter something of a paradox. As discussed, small-scale initiatives require the commitment of fewer resources, which might seem to limit risk. But small-scale initiatives may well fail to generate enough data to provide convincing evidence of success or failure. In this case, when the funder arrives at a decision juncture, it cannot make informed decisions about expanding, modifying, or shrinking the intervention. This is why attempting to reduce risk through diversification—that is to say, pursuing many small initiatives at once—rarely works. In effect, attempting to control risk by limiting the resources devoted to a risky program[16] may increase rather than decrease its inherent risk.

The ability to take the good paths and avoid the bad ones at each decision juncture applies not just to having adequate information and the capacity to process it, but also to the ability to reallocate resources from one use to another. The benefits of making firm commitments to staff and grantee entities are well known: It's easier to hire good people when you can offer job security, and it's harder for grantees to plan and control costs when they face uncertainty regarding their own funding. But there are also costs of such firm commitments: They are inflexible commitments; they reduce the flexibility to respond properly when circumstances indicate a reduction in resources is appropriate. The ROV approach assumes that funders can minimize downside risk by reducing or delaying future expenditures when emerging evidence tells them to do so. Interventions that allow for no such flexibility impose higher levels of risk.

Good program design requires attention to the risk implications of extended resource commitments, and these considerations should be part of the program design from the outset. Robin Hood gives only one-year grants, even though it expects to continue support for effective programs indefinitely. Even when it funds multiyear initiatives, Robin Hood retains the right to withdraw its funding after a year if the effort is failing. It thereby can cut its losses. That's been an important strategy for managing risks.

The ability to recalibrate interventions at decision junctures means not only that investors can reduce financial commitments when projects go sour, but also that investors can increase funding when projects exceed expectations. When funders are choosing whether to allocate their resources to one risky venture or another, they need to give serious attention to the question of whether the resources will really be there to take advantage of promising opportunities, not simply assume that resources will inevitably appear to support and expand what appears to be a promising innovative program. If a funder's assumptions about its ability to ramp up resources to promising programs are too optimistic, so too will be any estimates of upside program potential.

## Game Changers

There is a lot of enthusiasm in the nonprofit world right now for game changers, by which we mean interventions that succeed at a scale hitherto unimaginable. No discussion of philanthropic risk taking would be complete if it failed to discuss them. This section pins down a working definition of a philanthropic game changer and tackles the difficult question of the share of a funder's grant making that should go to potential game changers. We don't have neat answers. We aim to provoke conversation and debate.

What does a game changer mean in the philanthropic context? From the way people typically use the term, a game changer is something that radically alters a funder's impact. It's something more than a significant improvement. Game changers might be thought of as interventions that make a "sea change" in the extent to which the funder achieves its mission.

Here we encounter discomfiting questions. Would we describe an initiative as a game changer if it changed the behavior of many people and attracted support and adherents, but didn't improve mission-relevant outcomes? Would we describe an initiative as a game changer if it led to a total change in mission-relevant benefits, but those benefits were spread so thinly over a total population that there was little or no discernible impact on any given individual or group? Would we describe an initiative as a game changer if it led to a large short run increase in well-being but no long run improvement, or a short run improvement at the cost of actually worsening conditions in the long run?

These are not vapid questions. Many initiatives commonly cited as game changers, after careful scrutiny, fall into one or more of these less-than-spectacular categories. True philanthropic game changers may be far less common than philanthropists would like to believe, and accurately predicting which initiatives have real game changer prospects is nearly impossible.

Let's be clear. We aren't claiming that there are no initiatives that have provided durable and meaningful improvements in well-being. Health initiatives such as elimination of smallpox, control of polio, and expanded provision of HIV/AIDS medicines meet this standard. Arguably, government entitlements programs such as Social Security, Medicare, Medicaid, earned income tax credit, and food stamps, among others, meet the game changer standard. No doubt there are more. However, if we're to have a sensible approach to allocating resources in pursuit of game changers, we need to have a realistic assessment of the likelihood of actually achieving one.

Venture capitalists in the for-profit sector calculate a startup's prospects not just by asking what profits it would generate if it were successful, but also by identifying the various factors necessary for success and estimating or guesstimating the probability of each of them being in place when needed. Funders of prospective philanthropic ventures need to do the same. Consider, in an era of government retrenchment, a philanthropy-funded demonstration project that would require massive public funding to realize its game changer potential. That's a longshot, indeed. Or consider the game changer prospects of an innovative intervention designed to ameliorate poverty by working in elementary and secondary schools. Suppose that the "recipe" for producing an adult who has escaped poverty requires not only a good K–12 educational experience, but also a host of complementary services, including good prenatal and postnatal nutrition, proper health care, a nurturing family and community, avoiding teen parenthood, and having access to funding for postsecondary training and education. Suppose as well that affordable geographic proximity to jobs that pay a living wage is important. In the absence of any one or several of these important complements to a good K–12 experience, K–12 interventions may not do much good. The probability that such a bevy of necessary services be provided simultaneously may drive the probability that success will reach game changing dimensions to near zero.

Suppose game changers are longshots, with a low probability of success and enormous upside potential. How much should philanthropists spend on these longshots? Clearly there is a compelling argument for devoting some of society's resources to risky ventures with the potential for extremely high payoffs. The reasoning is straightforward. If the amounts invested per person are small, the individual risk per person is insignificant as well, and this is true even if the total amount spent on risky initiatives is pretty large in an absolute sense.

There is also a strong argument for private philanthropic funders, specifically, to be investing resources in pursuit of game changers. If for-profit businesses and government, together, are failing to commit the socially optimal amount of society's resources to pursuit of longshot game changers, then there is a void that nonprofit funders can fill. This may well be the case.

For-profit entities certainly do fund philanthropic activities, but there are reasons to believe that they may be skimping on the share devoted to initiatives with small chances of success. First, if an important part of the purpose of corporate philanthropy is in fact public relations, which includes community relations, then pursuit of public-good game changers, which means funding risky initiatives with a low probability of success, isn't likely to be an attractive option. There's too high a probability that in the end there will be no realized tangible benefits to the community— broadly or narrowly defined—to publicize. Second, at least some kinds of longshot initiatives are politically or socially controversial (think of HIV/AIDS prevention or family planning services for teenagers), and therefore not the kinds of ventures with which the typical for-profit would wish to be associated.

What about government? On the one hand, the government funds the majority of our society's basic research,[17] which certainly meets the definition of a low probability/high potential payoff activity. And some government initiatives, such as DARPA (the Defense Advanced Research Projects Agency)[18] and alternative energy programs, are specifically designed to fund more speculative endeavors. On the other hand, for the same reasons that private for-profits may avoid investing in longshot game changers—the need to point to tangible benefits to maintain goodwill and the desire to avoid controversial initiatives, especially controversial initiatives with a high probability of failure—government funding of game changers, especially certain categories of them, may be on the low side. Richard Marker, of New York University's Center for Philanthropy, makes this point.

> Private philanthropy should push alternatives which are not yet tested and not yet ready for the support from our tax dollars. There are always new ideas which need to be tested, analyzed, evaluated, re-tested, reconsidered—all of which provide new modes of addressing society's interests and problems. Only as they have proven themselves are they ready to be 'mainstreamed.' Let voluntary private philanthropy be the change agents and the risk capital for society; let voluntary private philanthropy take the risks of failure; let voluntary private philanthropy anticipate needs not yet fully understood and modes not yet proven.[19]

Let's assume that funders should be allocating some resources to the pursuit of game changers. The next question is, are they devoting too much or too little? There are forces pushing in both directions.

Perhaps the most powerful factor encouraging philanthropic pursuit of game changers is that they generate excitement. There is a world of difference between a solution and a salve, between solving a problem and softening the impact of one. Game changers make news; ordinary, solid, philanthropic efforts often do not. Donors are aware of this, so are those who direct the nonprofits they support, their boards, and the staff who work within them. A successful investment in a game changer can get a philanthropist or a funder in the headlines. For someone heading a funder or working within one, a game changer can get you, as an individual, labeled a game changer, and make your career. Even pursuing a game changer, whether or not it ultimately succeeds, can get a funder great press and all the good things that come with it. This produces a confluence of interests biased toward game changers. They serve the interests of donors and program officers, and because pursuit of game changers may serve as an effective means of attracting general donor support, even a funder that scrupulously allocates its funding to maximize the mission-relevant benefit of every dollar it spends might find it optimal to pursue longshots that, considered in isolation, have a negative expected value.

The forces we've described can encourage pursuit of game changers even when everyone involved has an accurate perception of the true probability of success. But there are forces at work as well that promote excessively optimistic beliefs regarding their likelihood of success. First, as psychologists and behavioral economists[20] have convincingly demonstrated, when people are making decisions that involve risk, they tend to systematically overestimate the true probability of very low probability events. There is no reason to believe that this would not apply to longshot gambles on game changers in the same way it applies to beliefs regarding the chances of winning the lottery.[21] Second, as sociologists who study "groupthink" have long discussed and documented, the more cautious, less optimistic, voices within organizations often are quashed or dismissed, especially when they express concerns regarding initiatives that have support from leadership.

Not every incentive that affects investment in risky initiatives pushes in the direction of excess. There are forces that push the other way, that is, toward being too timid. But such cautionary forces are characteristically weak in philanthropic circles. Consider first the problem of risk takers being unable to get their fair share of the rewards when a venture turns out well. In the private, for-profit sector, this is one of the most powerful factors discouraging innovative efforts. Not only is this the primary factor discouraging private business investment in basic research, but as all the articles about knockoffs and copyright infringement attest, it affects product development efforts as well because every sale lost to a copycat competitor translates to lower profit. However, it's hard to see this as a serious problem for risk philanthropy because profit isn't the objective. Indeed, if others copy a successful approach and run with it, so much the better, especially if the philanthropic trailblazer gets some kudos for the new approach.

Perhaps the only characteristic of funders, as compared with for-profit firms, that might make them more timid about risk taking is that taking risks is an integral part of operating in the for-profit sector, and deeply imbedded in its culture, while it is relatively new to the philanthropic world. This too may change if risk philanthropy becomes more the norm. Here is perhaps one harbinger: Robin Hood has entered into a partnership with the X Prize Foundation to create a series of competitions, with at least $1 million to go to the winners, to find innovative solutions to poverty. The idea is to harness crowd-sourced solutions from around the world. This is not a low-risk approach to philanthropy.

# 13

## Conclusion

We hold the following propositions to be self-evident:

1. Fulfilling philanthropic missions matters.
2. Philanthropic resources are limited.
3. Maximizing philanthropic success requires comparing the value of one philanthropic option to that of others.
4. The benefits produced by philanthropic initiatives come in many different forms; therefore, there is no natural measuring rod that can be used to compare the value of one philanthropic option against all others.

We hold the following proposition to be true although not self-evident:

5. A strategy that we've dubbed Relentless Monetization (RM) provides a straightforward and transparent way to compare the value of one philanthropic option against another, thereby providing a means for squeezing the most benefit from every philanthropic dollar, that is, a means for making smart philanthropic decisions.

This book provides the logical and empirical underpinnings for this fifth proposition. Although we document the use of RM by Robin Hood, the fundamental principles fully apply to other philanthropic purposes.

The power of RM lies in its consistent and persistent application of benefit/cost analysis. Implemented correctly, benefit/cost analysis:

- Factors in the preferences and values of funders, donors, policy-makers, and practitioners.
- Rivets the philanthropist's attention on outcomes, not inputs. The analysis does not focus on the number of people served—the number of enrollees in a job training program or students enrolled in an education program. Nor does RM focus on the cost of inputs (the cost per person served). Instead, the analysis focuses on the ultimate fate of the people served: how many of chronically unemployed trainees find and keep jobs (per dollar of cost) and how many high school dropouts earn diplomas and complete a year or two of college (per dollar of cost).
- Tells donors what they need to ask of nonprofits seeking money. Why not, as a potential donor, ask a nonprofit for specific proof of effectiveness along lines dictated by RM? Why not, as a potential donor, take the nonprofit's data and recalculate effectiveness to determine how well the nonprofit achieves *your* philanthropic goals (by contrast to the nonprofit's goals)? And why not, as a potential donor, fixate on the question answered by RM: What impact will *my* contemplated donation make, by contrast to the impact of all other donations to the same nonprofit?
- Takes into account the best practicably available evidence of the causal impact of interventions on mission-relevant outcomes. Best practicably available does not mean indisputably accurate. The best practicably available evidence may well be frustratingly thin and imprecise. Funders have no choice but to operate within the limits set by their budget and staff. With the help of the Internet, thinly staffed philanthropies can perform literature reviews in the service of implementing RM. Further, and importantly, if RM is practiced correctly, it builds in the best error correction process currently known: crowdsourcing. RM leaves a tangible and transparent trail of the processes and assumptions underlying funding decisions, exposure that allows funders to learn from each other how to make smarter decisions.

One implication deserves special attention. As briefly mentioned in chapter 1, the performance of U.S. philanthropies is, as a matter of law, accountable to no outside force. Because of this absence of accountability, it is possible for philanthropic decisions, whether made by corporations, households, legislatures, government agencies, or charities, to reflect little more than the political maneuvering, power politics, empire building, or personal biases of the folks who happen to be in charge. RM doesn't obliterate influence peddling. But by setting out the basis for decisions in an explicit manner, RM exposes them to external review and challenge. Managers who can't make a cogent case for their preferences lose out in the competition for resources.

This book does not argue that RM provides an easy route to correct decisions.

First, as the examples in chapters 6 and 7 indicated, the procedure is anything but easy. As we've emphasized, RM involves complexity and uncertain estimates. The framework relies on judgment. More precisely, RM relies on evidence-based judgment. We know no better basis for committing philanthropic resources.

Second, there's much, much more to be done. For starters, estimates of counterfactual variables, which are so central to implementing RM, remain crude. They need sharpening. Here's where philanthropists with different missions can help each other out because the counterfactual estimates they need often overlap. Second, practitioners of RM need to incorporate more intangible, nonpecuniary benefits into their analysis. Otherwise, practitioners risk steering resources to where they do the most concrete good but not, perhaps, where the resources do the most philanthropic good. The example we cited earlier, of the need to incorporate parental feelings of physical and psychological insecurity in the assessment of after school programs, is but one of many.

Finally, we reprise a caution expressed at several prior junctures. The arithmetic of benefit/cost ratios is essential. It captures at once subjective donor intent and objective evidence. It provides funders and nonprofits a powerful diagnostic tool by which to assess and improve their activities. But RM is bigger than arithmetic. It is more than chasing high ratios. It works best when supplemented by rich observation.

We hope we've convinced the reader that RM provides a sound basis by which philanthropists can practice a different, more powerful and, yes, smarter philanthropy. Americans make charitable contributions in excess of $300 billion a year, sky high by any international standard. Think how much more good could be accomplished if so large a sum were spent wisely and well.

# Appendix A

## Counterfactual Complications: Shared Responsibility

Two or more funders often cooperate with each other in funding activities of mutual grantees. That complicates the estimation of counterfactual outcomes.

Take a program that each year trains 15 women to set up day care programs in their homes. Let's assume, for simplicity, that each trainee: (1) graduates the training program; (2) follows through and sets up her home day care business; and (3) earns $4,000 more each year for 10 years than she would have earned had she not entered the training program—a total boost to the earnings of poor participants of $600,000 over 10 years, equal to $40,000 per trainee (ignoring discounting); (4) the program costs $5,000 per participant, or $75,000 in total; and (5) the costs are covered by two funders with Funder A covering 60 percent of the costs and Funder B covering 40 percent of the costs.

Each funder asks the same question: How much more money do these women earn because of its grant compared with what they would otherwise have earned? The answer depends entirely on circumstances.

***Circumstance 1: Proportionality/linearity and Funders A and B don't negotiate***

The program spends $75,000 to train 15 women, or $5,000 per woman. It creates $40,000 in benefits per graduate in the form of higher earnings.

If the program were to receive $5,000 less from its funders, it would train one fewer woman, cutting costs by $5,000 and cutting benefits by $40,000. In this highly scripted example, Funder A would take credit for only some of the grantee's success. It would calculate that it provides 60 percent of the costs ($45,000 of $75,000) and, because of the assumption of proportionality, would claim credit for 60 percent of the graduates (9 of 15) and 60 percent of the benefits ($360,000 = 9 × $40,000, which is 60 percent of $600,000). In a situation such as this, in the position of Funder A, Robin Hood would set 60 percent as the "Robin Hood factor." (More generally, a funder can call such a measure its "funder factor.") It captures the percentage of a grantee's total success that's created by the funder's donation (and that donation alone). In this example, if Funder A were to withdraw its $45,000 grant, then the program's total success as an income generator would fall by 60 percent.

*Circumstance 2: Nonlinearity and Funders don't negotiate*

Assume that if Funder A does not provide $45,000, then the program closes (say, because the program would not have enough money to pay rent on its facilities). In this case, the funder factor for Funder A would be 100 percent—all $600,000 of the program's total benefits would evaporate if Funder A were to withdraw its grant of $45,000 (regardless of the fact that $45,000 accounts for only 60 percent of total costs). By the way, Funder B would also calculate that total benefits would fall by 100 percent if it were to withdraw its 40 percent contribution. Both funders would be correct. If either withdrew its grant, total benefits would collapse by 100 percent (to zero from $600,000).

Note, no algebraic formulas connect Funder's A's calculations to those of Funder B. After all, each poses a different question. Funder A asks how its grant, all else being the same (including, given the assumption of no negotiations between the funders, Funder B's grant), would affect outcomes as Funder A measures them according to Funder A's mission. Funder B, on the other hand, poses the same question, except in its case, it assumes Funder A's grant stays the same and outcomes are measured according to Funder B's mission. Both can lay claim to the same benefits. Both can refuse to lay claim to other benefits. We see in this example that both funders can *correctly* claim responsibility for 100 percent of the grantee's success. This can be true whenever each funder provides money that proves necessary (although not sufficient) to outcomes. Because each grant is necessary for outcomes, withholding either grant drives benefits to zero. (For simplicity, this discussion assumes that Funder A places no value [meaning, no value related to Funder A's mission] on programs that Funder B would choose if the proposed joint project were to collapse. We make the same assumption about Funder B.)

*Circumstance 3: The funders negotiate with each other.*

In this case, Funder B tells Funder A that *if and only if* Funder A provides $45,000 will Funder B then provide $30,000. In this case Funder A will, here too, set its funder factor at 100 percent. If Funder A were to withhold its $45,000, funding for the grantee falls to zero and 100 percent of the $600,000 in total benefits will evaporate.

*Circumstance 4: Funders add new money and new restrictions.*

Let's assume that Funder A pledges an additional $5,000, raising its total grant to $50,000, if the grantee trains one more participant, raising total enrollment to 16 from 15. In this case, A's funder factor is 100 percent for the 16th participant—Funder A is 100 percent responsible for the extra graduate and, therefore, for extra benefits of $40,000 over 10 years. (Let's presume that A's funder factor remains 60 percent for the initial 15 participants.)

What's the point? For interventions in which there are multiple funders and responsibility for outcomes is inextricably shared among multiple parties, funders will be hard-pressed to figure out exactly what share of share of outcomes would not exist *but for* their grant—what we call their funder factor for the particular grant in question. But, as with the entire apparatus of counterfactual considerations, funders can't avoid tackling the problem if they want to make smart decisions. We have an obligation to try to do so, and to make explicit the assumptions that provide the basis for our figures.

# Appendix B
## Choices Between More
## and Less Risky Initiatives

This appendix uses four examples to illuminate the ways in which a funder's resources, the nature of the initiatives it funds, the discount rate it uses to value future benefits, and the characteristics of its target population all interact to affect how much its choices between more and less risky initiatives are likely to make a significant difference in the well-being of its target population.

We can describe funders on the basis of a number of attributes that together determine how much their resource allocation decisions are likely to affect their beneficiaries' well-being.

- Funders may have smaller or greater amounts of resources to spend.
- Funders may allocate those resources in the interest of larger or smaller populations.
- Funders may have target populations that live in desperate poverty or are somewhat better situated.
- Funders' focus may be such that they provide a service to any given member of their target population only once in a long while, or they may provide services to each member every year.
- Funders' services (or those of the grantees they fund) may yield their clients one-time benefits or benefits that accrue over many years.

- Funders' missions may be such that, at best, the benefit/cost ratio on their expenditures is constrained to be modest or they may be in the fortunate position of having the potential to achieve great benefits per dollar spent.

Depending on the particular mix of these attributes, the maximum *potential* impact of a funder on the well-being of a typical member of its target population will either be small or large. As a funder's impact on its typical beneficiary becomes larger, risk considerations should become a more important part of the deliberation process that determines its resource allocation. Our examples are intended to span the range from insignificant risk to risk-too-important-to-ignore. Ideally, any given funder should be able to fathom where it lies within that range and use the information to appropriately calibrate the attention it should give to risk when it allocates its resources among competing initiatives.

*Example 1*

Consider a funder with the following characteristics:

- It has just $1 million to spend.
- It must spend it all in one year.
- It must spend that money to benefit a target population of 10,000.
- Each member of the target population earns $20,000 per year.
- It must spread the money evenly across all members of the target population.
- It spends its money in a manner such that the benefits accrue over ten years and such that the benefit takes the form of an equal-sized annual increment to the $20,000 annual income of each member of the target population over that ten-year period.
- With "safe" Program X, it achieves a benefit/cost ratio of 8 on the money it spends.

The first thing to notice is that with $1 million to spend and a target population of 10,000 people over which to spread the funding, the spending per person is just $100. The second thing to notice is that because the benefit of the money spent accrues evenly over ten years, the benefit in any given year is just one-tenth the total benefit.

Discounting of benefits accruing in the future also matters. As discussed previously, benefits that accrue further in the future are considered less valuable than those that accrue sooner; therefore, the present value of any annual benefits accruing later in the ten-year period will be lower than those accruing earlier. Suppose we use a discount rate of 3 percent in calculating the present discounted value (PDV) of the full ten-year flow of benefits. That would mean that the PDV of the ten-year *annual* benefit flow per person (which we'll call *b*), is given by the formula:

$$PDV = b/(1.03) + b/(1.03)^2 + b/(1.03)^3 + b/(1.03)^4 + b/(1.03)^5$$
$$+ b/(1.03)^6 + b/(1.03)^7 + b/(1.03)^8 + b/(1.03)^9 + b/(1.03)^{10}$$

Given the $100 per person expenditure, how large would the annual increment to income, *b*, have to be for the benefit/cost ratio per dollar spent to be 8? (A benefit/cost ratio of 8, by the way, is not shabby.) A little work with a standard spreadsheet program yields the result that the annual income increment comes to roughly $94.

Now suppose that we give this funder a choice between two different ways to spend its $100 per person. Program X yields the benefit flow and benefit/cost ratio we have just described. Program Y yields benefits that accrue in the same manner as the first way (equal amount per person, equal increments to annual income over ten years, etc.), but now the benefit/cost ratio involves risk. Specifically, with Program Y there is a 50 percent chance that things will work out well and the benefit/cost ratio will be 14, implying an annual income increment of $164, but also a 50 percent chance that the results will be disappointing, with a benefit/cost ratio of only 4, implying an annual income increment of just $47.[1] With 50–50 odds of the two outcomes, the expected value of the benefit/cost ratio for Program Y is 9 and the expected annual increment to income is about $105.[2]

The expected value of the annual income increment under riskier Program Y is higher than that of safe Program X, but there is the 50 percent chance that the annual income increment will be the more disappointing value of $47 to take into account. If you make your choice so as to maximize the expected *utility* (well-being) of the typical member of your target population, then your best choice depends on how much more utility attaches to each extra dollar of income between $20,047 and $20,094 as compared with the utility attaching to each extra dollar of income between $20,094 and $20,164. If they are roughly the same, as seems very likely, then choosing riskier Program Y, which is the choice that maximizes expected income, will also maximize expected utility. But suppose, for the sake of argument, that every dollar between $20,047 and $20,094 yields *twice* the increment to utility of every dollar between

$20,094 and $20,164 (implying, unrealistically, that the value of money falls off very steeply after annual income reaches $20,094). In this case, safer Program X would be the better choice. Why? Because, relative to the utility improvement obtained from safe Program X, the 50 percent chance of the sacrifice of utility if Program Y turned out to be disappointing would outweigh the 50 percent chance of the increase in utility if Program Y turned out well.

Of course, it is hard to see why the utility that attaches to dollars of income between $20,047 and $20,094 would in fact be much different, if perceptibly different at all, from the utility that attaches to dollars between $20,094 and $20,164. The $94 of annual benefit from Program X is not even half a percent of the $20,000 base income of the target population, and the *differences* between the safe outcome of Program X and either the good or the disappointing outcomes of Program Y are even less significant relative to income. We are dealing with small differences in small differences here. There is no reason why they should weigh heavily.

The useful lesson here, summarized in chapter 12, is this: If a funder's mission, resources, and opportunities for spending are such that its initiatives have only a modest *percentage* impact on the living standard of its target population, then as long as the initiatives themselves cannot cause nontrivial harm, the funder should not worry about the riskiness of the initiatives it funds. This suggests that most small funders, except perhaps those who have chosen to serve a very small target population or have found a way to achieve extremely high benefit/cost ratios on the initiatives they fund, are probably exempt from having to concern themselves with anything other than the expected benefit/cost ratio when allocating their scarce resources. (If your funder falls in this category, you are free to go now.)

Let's now move on to examples that successively up the ante when it comes to risk.

### Example 2

We will keep all the features of the previous scenario except four, which we'll highlight using italic type, underlining the specific details we have altered:

- *It has $5 million to spend.*
- It must spend it all in one year.
- It must spend that money to benefit a target population of 10,000.
- *Each member of the target population earns $10,000 per year.*

- It must spread the money evenly across all members of the target population.
- It spends its money in a manner such that the benefits accrue over ten years and the benefit takes the form of an equal-sized annual increment to the $10,000 annual income of each member of the target population over that ten-year period.
- *With "safe" Program X, it achieves a benefit/cost ratio of 12 on the money it spends.*
- With *"risky" Program Y, it has a 50 percent chance of achieving a benefit/cost ratio of 6 and a 50 percent chance of achieving a benefit/ cost ratio of 21 on the money it spends.*

The changes we've made have all had the effect of increasing the size of the funder's impact relative to the income of the members of the target population. We have increased fivefold the spending per individual in the target population, from $100 to $500;[3] we have proportionately scaled up benefit/cost ratios of Program X and Program Y by 50 percent; and we have assumed that the base income of each member of the target population is $10,000 rather than $20,000. The higher spending per person and the higher benefit/cost ratio mean that safe Program X increases the annual income of each member of the target population by 7.5 times as large an amount as that in Example 1 (5 times the money × 1.5 times the impact per dollar spent), and because the base income is only half as large, the *percentage* impact on income is fifteen times as large. With these changes, Program X will increase the annual income of each member of the target population from $10,000 to $10,703 for each of the ten years over which the benefits will accrue, a substantial amount relative to an income of $10,000, whereas Program Y offers a 50 percent chance of raising annual income from $10,000 to $10,352 and a 50 percent chance of raising income to $11,231.

As in Example 1, the expected value of the income gain from riskier Program Y is greater—$791 versus $703—but there is more at stake on the downside. If Program Y turns out to yield the lower of its two possible values, then compared with going with safe Program X, each member of the target population loses out by about $350 per year, about 3.5 percent of a base income of $10,000.

Should the funders ignore risk and pursue the choice with the greater expected benefit? When your annual income is only $10,000, the change in utility from every extra dollar between $10,352 and $10,703 (a difference of about $30 per month on a very low base) might actually be nontrivially higher than the utility improvement attached to every dollar between $10,703 and $11,231. It's a tough call.

There are some interesting implications to be derived from this example. First, all else equal, the more needy the population served by a funder, the more attention the funder should give to the riskiness of the programs it funds. Second, the greater the resources available to a funder and the more effectively it can allocate those resources, and therefore the more its potential impact for good, the more it may have to take risk into consideration in its funding decisions. And third, if we imagine a world in which small funders that are able to spend money effectively (by following the advice in this book!) will grow even more efficient and attract greater donor support over time, those funders should plan for the transition from an environment in which they can ignore risk to one in which they can no longer do so.

### Example 3

Now let's raise the stakes still further. Suppose that we take our Example 2, but instead of assuming that the funder has $5 million to spend, *all of which it spends in one year* to provide a *one-time* expenditure of $500 for each member of the target population, let us assume that the funder now has the resources to spend $500 on each member *each and every year*, and further assume that *all* the benefits of each year's spending accrue within the year in which it is spent rather than accrue over time. (We again use italics to show the changes from the previous example.)

- The funder has $5 million to spend *each year*.
- It must spend that money to benefit a target population of 10,000.
- Each member of the target population earns $10,000 per year.
- It must spread the money evenly across all members of the target population.
- *It spends its money in a manner such that all the benefits accrue within the year in which the money is spent.*
- With "safe" Program X, it achieves a benefit/cost ratio of 12 on the money it spends.
- With "risky" Program Y, it has a 50 percent chance of achieving a benefit/cost ratio of 6 and a 50 percent chance of achieving a benefit/cost ratio of 21 on the money it spends.

With $5 million to spend *each year*, the timing of the flow of benefits can become relevant. We have assumed for simplicity here that all the benefits of each year's spending accrue within the year the spending occurs, but we should note that with a constant rate of annual spending, the annual increment in income becomes the same no matter whether the benefits accrue within the calendar year or over time.[4] In Example 3, the funder's choice is now between safe Program X, which would boost income from $10,000 to $16,000 per year, and riskier Program Y, which offers a 50 percent chance of raising income from $10,000 to $13,000 and a 50 percent chance of raising it to $20,500. The latter figure is tantalizing because it comes very close to closing the "poverty gap," but consider this: If the members of the target population end up with the lesser outcome of Program Y, the sacrifice of utility relative to safe Program X is very large indeed. In situations like this, when we're discussing a funder whose program choices make differences of 30 percent and more in the income for the target population, it is hard to take the position that the funder should focus on expected value exclusively and ignore risk altogether.

Our third example has some other important implications as well. First, for any given ratio of benefits to costs a funder is able to achieve, the shorter the time horizon over which those benefits accrue, the greater the short term impact of its spending relative to income for its target population, and therefore the more risk considerations should come into play in resource allocation. Second, to the extent that a funder makes expenditures on behalf of a relatively unchanging target population, and to the extent that the benefits of those expenditures accrue over several years, it is the differences in the *cumulative* impact of its expenditures on annual income that determine how much consideration must be given to matters of risk. And third, of course, is that risk considerations probably should not be ignored by any funders whose operations have a profound impact on the well-being of its target population.

### Example 4

Let us now introduce another complication. We couched our discussion of the previous example in terms of the potential impact of program choice on *each member* of the target population. But suppose that the target population is equally divided between two subgroups, one of which has an income of $5,000 and the other of $15,000, and suppose that the dollar impact of Program X and Program Y, whatever the latter turns out to be, is the same for the two population subgroups. (We once again use italics to show the changes from the previous example.)

- The funder has $5 million to spend each year.
- It must spend that money to benefit a target population of 10,000.

- *Half the members of the target population earn $5,000 per year and half earn $15,000 per year.*
- It must spread the money evenly across all members of the target population.
- It spends its money in a manner such that all the benefits accrue within the year in which the money is spent.
- With "safe" Program X, it achieves a benefit/cost ratio of 12 on the money it spends.
- With "risky" Program Y, it has a 50 percent chance of achieving a benefit/cost ratio of 6 and a 50 percent chance of achieving a benefit/cost ratio of 21 on the money it spends.

In this situation, focusing on the expected dollar benefit of Program Y is likely more questionable than was the case in Example 3. The reason becomes apparent when we focus closely on the distinction between expected utility and expected income. If each extra dollar of income brings us a little less extra utility as our income rises, it is also true that each successive reduction in income hurts us by a larger amount as our income falls. And even though it is not possible to "compare utility" across individuals, we should recognize that if Program Y delivers the less satisfactory of its two possible outcomes, then the poorer part of the target population, those with $5,000 income, would experience a *dramatic* reduction in utility relative to what they would experience with Program X. In effect, when the target population is itself heterogeneous, the impact of resource allocation decisions on an "*average member*" of the target population is not equal to the *average impact* on the actual members of the target population.

This is not a far-fetched consideration. Suppose for instance, as is almost certain to be the case in the real world, that the reason some members of the target population have the lower income and some have the higher income is that some experience "bad breaks" and some experience "good breaks." These bad or good breaks could take the form of the presence or absence of spells of unemployment and so directly affect earned income, but with equivalent effect, they could also take the form of uninsured medical expenses, losses suffered as a result of crime, or any of the myriad other ways in which chance events can affect our "real income" within the course of a year. The greater the uncertainty surrounding the real income of the individual members of the target population, the more important are the concerns raised by Example 4.

We don't intend to suggest with this last example that a funder needs to conduct an exhaustive analysis of the impact of its programs on each and every subgroup within its target population. However, Example 4 does suggest that even when the impact of a funder's initiatives on a hypothetical *average* member of its target population seems to conform more closely to Example 2 rather than Example 3, it may nevertheless be prudent to give some consideration to the risk implications of program funding decisions.

Every funder is different. Most funders do not have to worry about the risk they impose on their target population through their funding decisions. But for those that do, these four examples should provide a guide to the circumstances that might signal the need for concern.

# Appendix C
## Calculating a Program's Expected Well-being Impact

We begin with the same numerical example described in chapter 12. To make it easier to follow the example, we repeat the details of the example here. Assume that a funder has a total annual budget of $5 million to spend, and it has winnowed its spending options to three potential program grants, each of which serves the members of its target population and each of which, individually, would exhaust its $5 million annual program budget: a "safe" financial literacy program, a "risky" job training program, and a "riskier" nutrition education.

The remaining assumptions are as follows:

- The funder has a target population of 10,000 on which to spend its $5 million.
- Each member of the target population earns $10,000 per year.
- The funder must spread the money evenly across all members of the target population, meaning it spends $500 on each of them each year.
- It spends its money in a manner such that *all* the benefits accrue *within the year* in which the money is spent.
- The "safe" financial literacy program achieves a sure benefit/cost ratio of 12.

- The "risky" job training program has a 50 percent chance of achieving a benefit/cost ratio of 6 and a 50 percent chance of achieving a benefit/cost ratio of 21.
- The "riskier" nutrition education program has a 10 percent probability of a benefit/cost ratio of 2, a 40 percent probability of a benefit/cost ratio of 6, a 40 percent probability of a benefit/cost ratio of 21, and a 10 percent probability of a benefit/cost ratio of 30.

What's next? Having narrowed the field to the best three program options and described the probability of each benefit/cost ratio being achieved for each of them, the next task is to come up with an index level[1] for how much well-being is associated with a dollar of income for the typical target population individual at each income level within the range of outcomes spanned by the programs under consideration. In the second column of table C.1, we have (strictly for explanatory purposes) assumed that the average well-being per dollar of income falls from a value of 1 at an income of $10,000 to a value just above 0.5 at an income of $25,000. The entry in each row of the third column of table C.1 is the product of the dollar income for that row and the well-being per dollar of income, and therefore shows well-being index level at each of the levels of dollar income. (All the incomes are

Table C.1
Well-being at Each Income Level

| Income Level | Well-being/$ at This Income Level | Well-being at This Income Level |
| --- | --- | --- |
| $10,000 | 1.00 | 10000 |
| $11,000 | 0.94 | 10340 |
| $12,000 | 0.89 | 10680 |
| $13,000 | 0.84 | 10920 |
| $14,000 | 0.80 | 11200 |
| $15,000 | 0.76 | 11400 |
| $16,000 | 0.73 | 11680 |
| $17,000 | 0.70 | 11900 |
| $18,000 | 0.67 | 12060 |
| $19,000 | 0.65 | 12350 |
| $20,000 | 0.62 | 12400 |
| $20,500 | 0.61 | 12505 |
| $21,000 | 0.60 | 12600 |
| $22,000 | 0.58 | 12760 |
| $23,000 | 0.56 | 12880 |
| $24,000 | 0.54 | 12960 |
| $25,000 | 0.52 | 13000 |

within the range of the possible target population individuals' post-program incomes generated by our three programs, taking into account both the base income and the monetized value of the program benefit.)

The next steps of the process, illustrated in table C.2, allow us to calculate the expected post-program dollar income and the expected post-program well-being for each program. We'll work through the financial literacy program and the job training program, after which the nutrition education program should be self-explanatory.

The financial literacy program (our "sure thing") has only one possible benefit/cost ratio, therefore only one row. With a benefit/cost ratio of 12, the expected income here is $16,000 (the only possible value for this program) and our well-being index (from table C.1) is 11680. The job training program has two possible outcomes, and therefore two rows, one for a benefit/cost ratio of 6 and one for a benefit/cost ratio of 21, each with a 50 percent chance of occurring. With $500 spent per capita, the monetized program benefit is $3,000 if the benefit/cost ratio is 6, and $10,500 if the benefit/cost ratio is 21. Given that each target individual has a base income of $10,000, this means that post-program income has a 50 percent chance of being $13,000 and a 50 percent chance of being $20,500. For each of the two possible benefit/cost ratios, column 4 gives the probability of the benefit/cost ratio occurring (0.5) times the post-program income associated with that outcome. (This figure does not have an obvious intuitive meaning.) Column 5 in each row is equal to the post-program income for that benefit/cost ratio multiplied by the well-being per dollar (from table C.1) for that income level, all multiplied by the probability of that benefit/cost ratio occurring. To find the expected post-program *income* (for the typical target population individual) for the job training program, we sum the column 4 figures in the two rows (one row for each of the two possible outcomes) we have for the job training program to arrive at $16,750. To find the expected *well-being* associated with the job training program, we sum the column 5 figures for the two rows to arrive at 11712. Our nutrition education program has four rows, but the process is the same as for our job training program. Here, when we take the sum of the column 4 figures over the four rows, we get an expected income of $17,000, which is higher than either of the other two programs. However, when we take the sum of the column 5 figures, we see that expected well-being is 11704, which is better than the financial literacy program but *lower* than the job training program.

The bottom line is that under our assumptions, the job training program is the best choice from the perspective of maximizing the expected well-being of the target population.

Table C.2

Expected Income and Expected Well-being from Each of the Three Programs

| 1 | 2 | 3 | 4 | 5 |
|---|---|---|---|---|
| | | Financial Literacy Program | | |
| Program Benefit/Cost Ratio | Post-Program Income for Benefit/Cost Ratio | Probability of Outcome | Probability × Income | Probability × Income × Well-being/$ |
| 12 | $16,000 | 1 | $16,000 | 11680 |
| | | Expected Income | $16,000 | |
| | | Expected Well-being | | 11680 |
| | | Jobs Training Program | | |
| Program Benefit/Cost Ratio | Post-Program Income for Benefit/Cost Ratio | Probability of Outcome | Probability × Income | Probability × Income × Well-being/$ |
| 6 | $13,000 | 0.5 | $6,500 | 5460 |
| 21 | $20,500 | 0.5 | $10,250 | 6252 |
| | | Expected Income | $16,750 | |
| | | Expected Well-being | | 11712 |
| | | Job Nutrition Education Program | | |
| Program Benefit/Cost Ratio | Post-Program Income for Benefit/Cost Ratio | Probability of Outcome | Probability × Income | Probability × Income × Well-being/$ |
| 2 | $11,000 | 0.1 | $1,100 | 1034 |
| 6 | $13,000 | 0.4 | $5,200 | 4368 |
| 21 | $20,500 | 0.4 | $8,200 | 5002 |
| 30 | $25,000 | 0.1 | $2,500 | 1300 |
| | | Expected Income | $17,000 | |
| | | Expected Well-being | | 11704 |

# NOTES

## 1. Overview of Relentless Monetization

1. When benefits and costs are generated well into the future, proper economic accounting calls for estimating present discounted values. This topic is dealt with in chapter 5.

2. Our simple formulation assumes that philanthropists can expand and contract the size of their grant at will—a technical issue that does not distort matters at this stage of the argument. This issue is dealt with at length in chapters 8 and 9.

3. May 15, 2011 interview with Caroline Preston; e-mail from Herbert Sturz, May 20, 2011, 10:07 A.M.

4. New York University–Stern Conference on Social Entrepreneurship, February 2008.

## 2. Translating Mission Into Mission-Relevant Outcomes

1. See Lane Kenworthy, Jessica Epstein, and Daniel Duerr, "Rising Tides, Redistribution, and the Material Well-being of the Poor," September 15, 2007, http://www.golden.polisci.ucla.edu/wgwppis/kenworthy.pdf.

2. Nothing prevents an environment oriented nonprofit and a poverty fighting nonprofit to jointly fund interventions that accomplish each mission better than the nonprofits could do on their own.

# 3. Basics of Monetizing Outcomes

1. Cynthia E. Lamy, manager of metrics at Robin Hood, developed some of the figures cited in this chapter.

2. To provide a flavor of how QALY weights are assigned, here are sample values from one often-cited system, known as EQ-5D (as reported in Phillips, C., and G. Thompson. 2009. *What Is a QALY?* London: Hayward Medical Communications).

> Health state 11111. No problems. Valuation = 1.0 perfect health.
>
> Health state 22222. Some problems walking about; some problems washing or dressing self; some problems with performing usual activities; moderate pain or discomfort; moderately anxious or depressed. Valuation = 0.516 perfect health.
>
> Health state 23322. Some problems walking about; unable to wash or dress self; unable to perform usual activities; moderate pain or discomfort; moderately anxious or depressed. Valuation = 0.079 perfect health.

3. Lawrence, Bryan R. 2012. "Health Care: Spend Less, Live Longer," *The Washington Post,* July 27, 2012; Brent, Robert J. 2003. *Cost-Benefit Analysis and Health Care Evaluations.* Cheltenham, UK: Edward Elgar Publishing.

4. The previously discussed example of grants that affect high school graduation rates is the exception. There, as we noted, there is high quality research that carefully distinguishes the impact of earnings from that on health. The research community has solved the problem of double counting in this instance, but for many other grants, the research literature is not nearly as accommodating.

# 4. Those Pesky Counterfactuals

1. In this example, we're counting as a benefit only earnings gains for graduates of the job training programs. In a complete analysis, the funder would need to estimate whether training women to set up day care programs generates long-term poverty-related benefits for the enrolled children.

2. Greenberg, D., V. Deitch, and G. Hamilton. 2010. "A Synthesis of Random Assignment Benefit-Cost Studies of Welfare-to-Work Programs." *Journal of Benefit-Cost Analysis* 1 (1): 1–28; MacGuire, S., J., Freely, C., Clymer, M. Conway, and D. Schwartz. 2010. *Findings from the Sectoral Employment Impact Study.* Philadelphia: Public/Private Ventures; MDRC. 2007. *Welfare-to-Work Program Benefits and Costs: A Synthesis of Research.* New York: MDRC; Schochet, P., and J. Burghardt. 2008. "Do Job Corps Performance Measures Track Program Impacts?" *Journal of Policy Analysis and Management* 27 (3): 556–576.

## 6. Examples of Metrics by Outcome

1. Cynthia E. Lamy, manager of metrics at Robin Hood, researched many of the figures cited in this Chapter 7 has the notation. chapter.

2. Deming, David, and Susan Dynarski. 2009. "College Aid." In *Targeting Investments in Children: Fighting Poverty When Resources Are Limited*, edited by Phillip B. Levine and David J. Zimmerman, 283–302. Chicago: University of Chicago Press.

3. "Getting Serious About the GED: How New York Can Build a Bridge from High School Drop-out to Postsecondary Success," Albany, New York: Schuyler Center for Analysis and Advocacy, 2009. Also, "College Readiness of New York City's GED Recipients," CUNY Office of Institutional Research and Assessment, Table 10, 2008. Jacobsen, L. and C. Mokher 2009. *Pathways to Boosting the Earnings of Low-Income Students by Increasing Their Educational Attainment*. Prepared for the Bill & Melinda Gates Foundation by the Hudson Institute and CAN Analysis & Solutions.

4. Levin, H., C. Belfied, P. Muennig, and C. Rouse 2007. "The Costs and Benefits of an Excellent Education for All of America's Children," Teachers College, Columbia University, Table 3.1. Also, Baum, S., J. Ma, and K. Payea 2010. "Education Pays 2010. The Benefits of Higher Education for Individuals and Society, Trends in Higher Education Series. CollegeBoard Advocacy and Policy Center".

## 7. Examples of Metrics by Grant: Multi-Outcome Inverventions

1. Cynthia E. Lamy, manager of metrics at Robin Hood, researched many of the figures cited in this chapter.

## 11. Prominent Metrics Systems

1. Tuan, M. T. 2008. *Profiles of Eight Integrated Cost Approaches to Measuring and/ or Estimating Social Value Creation*. Seattle, WA: Bill & Melinda Gates Foundation.

2. Tuan, M. T. 2008. *Profiles of Eight Integrated Cost Approaches to Measuring and/or Estimating Social Value Creation*. Seattle, WA: Bill & Melinda Gates Foundation. Brest, P., and H. Harvey. 2008. *Money Well Spent: A Strategic Plan for Smart Philanthropy*. New York: Bloomberg Press. 2008. *Making Every Dollar Count (How Expected Return Can Transform Philanthropy)*. Menlo Park, CA: William and Flora Hewlett Foundation.

3. We won't go into great detail on every aspect of what Charity Navigator does, but that information is readily available on its Web site.

## 12. Reflections on Risk

1. We define the "expected benefit" of a project in more detail in the next section, but loosely, if we think of the project as an experiment for which there are many trials, each with an uncertain outcome, then the expected benefit is the average benefit obtained over many trials.

2. Strictly speaking there is a distinction between "risk" and "uncertainty." "Risk" applies to situations in which we know the probability that attaches to each possible outcome, and "uncertainty" to situations in which we do not have enough information even to do that. We are going to keep it simple and use the term "risk" even when a formalist might argue that the true situation is actually one characterized by uncertainty.

3. Formally, the expected benefit of a project is a sum of terms, each of which consists of a possible outcome of the project multiplied by the probability that the particular outcome occurs. So, the expected benefit of a project with a 40 percent probability of yielding a $1,000 benefit and a 60 percent probability of yielding a $2,000 benefit is $1,600 (= 0.4 × $1,000 + 0.6 × $2,000).

4. This question is discussed in the more general context of "policy making" in Harrison, G. 2011. "Experimental Methods and the Welfare Evaluation of Policy Lotteries." Paper presented as the plenary address at the Congress of the European Association of Agricultural Economists, Zurich, August 30 to September 2, 2011: *Change and Uncertainty—Challenges for Agriculture, Food and Natural Resources.*

5. A corollary worth mentioning: If a funder's mission is such that there is no easily defined target population for example, if the funder's chosen mission is to fund basic research into disease prevention—then there are no target population risk preferences to take into account, and the appropriate approach is to allocate resources so as to maximize the expected gain. We thank an anonymous reader of a draft of the book for bringing this issue to our attention.

6. We recognize that penguins and protozoa don't earn dollar incomes. In cases like this, the appropriate rule might be in terms of territorial range, rate of population growth, habitat area, and so on.

7. The level of an individual's aversion to risk is a reflection of the relationship between the level of income and the level of well-being for that individual.

8. See for example, Harrison, G. (2011), and sources cited therein.

9. It's also worth reiterating here that allocating resources to riskier philanthropic initiatives might not reduce the resources available for other, reliably successful ones at all, and indeed might even increase those resources, if taking on some high-risk projects serves to substantially increase overall donor support. Needless to say, this excuse for taking risks can be abused, but it can also be an entirely legitimate consideration.

10. Appendix B works through four examples that should help funders know when their impact per capita on target individuals is small enough to safely ignore risk exposure issues. (Full disclosure: The appendix goes into some detail, and not everyone will find it thrilling reading, but we think it provides a very useful guide for those who actually have to make the hard choices.)

11. Dollar benefits here would include the monetized value of health improvements and other, similar, mission-relevant outcomes.

12. Having more possible outcomes complicates the arithmetic but doesn't change the technique for calculating the expected value, which is to multiply each possible program outcome by the probability that it will occur and then take the sum of the values obtained. The following table shows that calculation for the nutrition program.

| Probability | B/C Ratio | Probability × B/C Ratio |
|---|---|---|
| 10% | 2 | 0.2 |
| 40% | 6 | 2.4 |
| 40% | 21 | 8.4 |
| 10% | 30 | 3 |
| | SUM | 14 |

13. Our discussion of this topic has benefited greatly from insights provided in Borison, A. 2002. "Real Options Analysis: Where are the Emperor's Clothes?" *Journal of Applied Corporate Finance* 2005 17(2): 17–31; Dixit, A. and R. Pindyck. 1994. *Investment Under Uncertainty*, Princeton, NJ: Princeton University Press; Fortunato M. 1989. "Strategic Options." Paper presented at the International Symposium of Professional Financial Consultants. Dallas, TX, March, 1989; Luehrman, T. A. 1998. "Investment Opportunities as Real Options: Getting Started on the Numbers." *Harvard Business Review* July–August, 3–15; Luehrman, T. A. 1998. "Strategy as a Portfolio of Real Options." *Harvard Business Review*, September–October, 89–99.

14. ROV is also referred to ROA (real options analysis). Same thing.

15. *A caveat:* There is no such thing as a free lunch. Adopting the ROV approach to evaluate risky initiatives is not a trivial exercise. Doing what is necessary to make the right path at each decision juncture requires planning and both organizational and financial resources. If the gap between the best and the worst possible outcomes of most of a funder's initiatives is not that great to begin with, the benefit of trying to apply an ROV approach is not likely to justify its cost.

16. This applies both to resources relating to program scale and resources dedicated to program evaluation. As we mentioned earlier in this book, operating "lean and mean" is fine, but there is no benefit to being too malnourished to think straight.

17. In fact, the combined activities of government, higher educational institutions, and other funders accounted for more than 80 percent of all basic research expenditures in 2008. See "The Pivotal Role of Government Investment in Basic Research," Report by the U.S. Congress Joint Economic Committee, Representative Carolyn B. Maloney, Chair, Senator Charles E. Schumer, Vice Chair, Prepared by the Majority Staff of the Joint Economic Committee, May 2010.

18. DARPA is the Defense Advanced Research Projects Agency, an agency whose purpose is to support basic scientific research that might contribute to US military capabilities. DARPA-financed basic research has proved to have great value beyond the

military sphere, including the research that led to the development of the Internet. See http://www.darpa.mil/About/History/History.aspx.

19. See Richard Marker's comments at http://wisephilanthropy.blogspot.com/2007/07/societys-risk-capital-or-safety-net.html.

20. Prelec, D. 1998. "The Probability Weighting Function." *Econometrica*, 66, 3: 497–527.

21. Donors, the people who fund funders and who not infrequently sit on their boards, may well be particularly optimistic in their views of risk taking. Those who have made their own fortunes have almost certainly done so by taking risks. The fact that their own risk taking has worked out well is likely to have left them with a positive view of risk taking in general.

## Appendix B

1. The $164 figure = $(14/8) \times \$94$; the $47 = $(4/8) \times \$94$.

2. The expected B/C ratio comes from weighting each of the two outcomes by the probability of it occurring. In this case, the two weights are equal to 0.5.

$$0.5 \times 4 + 0.5 \times 14 = 2 + 7 = 9$$

3. We have done this by increasing the funder's total spending. We could have accomplished the same thing by reducing the target population from 10,000 to 2,000.

4. Imagine that we are in year 10 of operation under the second assumption. If under the assumption that all benefits accrue within the spending year, the annual income increment per member of the target population under Program X would be $6,000 (= $12 \times \$500$), then under the assumption that the benefits of each year's spending accrue evenly over a ten year period, then in year 10 it will be 10 times $6,000/10 = $6,000 as well because the benefit in year 10 will be the sum of all the benefits still accruing from each of the annual expenditures made over the previous 10 years.

## Appendix C

1. Note that the index numbers are not meant to be some observable measure of well-being. It is the rate at which well-being per dollar falls with income that matters, not the absolute numbers. Indeed, nothing changes in our example if all the index numbers are scaled up or down by some common multiple.

# INDEX